# THE
# HARVEST

## RICK JOYNER

Whitaker House

Unless otherwise indicated, all Scripture quotations are taken from the *New American Standard Bible*, (NAS) © 1960, 1962, 1968, 1971, 1973, 1975, 1977 by The Lockman Foundation. Used by permission.

Scripture quotations marked (NKJ) are from the *New King James Version*, © 1979, 1980, 1982, 1984 by Thomas Nelson, Inc. Used by permission.

Scripture quotations marked (NIV) are from the Holy Bible, *New International Version*, © 1973, 1978, 1984 by the International Bible Society. Used by permission.

**THE HARVEST**

Rick Joyner
MorningStar Publications
16000 Lancaster Highway
Charlotte, NC 28277
1-800-542-0278

ISBN: 0-88368-503-5
Printed in the United States of America
Copyright © 1989, 1993 by Rick Joyner
1997 Printing

Whitaker House
30 Hunt Valley Circle
New Kensington, PA 15068

Library of Congress Cataloging-in-Publication Data

Joyner, Rick 1949–
        The harvest / Rick Joyner.
                p.      cm.
        Originally published: Pineville, NC : MorningStar Publications, © 1989.
        ISBN 0-88368-503-5 (tradepbk. : alk. paper)
        1. Church renewal—Miscellanea. 2. End of the world—Miscellanea.
3. Visions.    I. Title.
BV600.2.J69  1997
248.2'9—dc21                                        97-15853

4 5 6 7 8 9 10 11 12 / 06 05 04 03 02 01 00 99 98 97

# CONTENTS

PART II
# KINGDOM AUTHORITY

# Introduction

To properly understand this vision, it must be kept in mind that it represents a *gradual* unfolding which takes place over a period of time, possibly many years. Though I was not given the timing of these events some of them have taken place since the first edition was published. Whether the complete unfolding takes five years or fifty I do not know, but I do know that even if it takes fifty we do not have any time to waste in preparing for these events.

## How the Vision Was Received

As I am often asked to describe the "experience" in which I received this vision, I will try to do it briefly here. The main panorama of this vision came in three parts: the first in September 1987, the second in May 1988, the third in September 1988. Between these dates, and since, I received numerous "revelations" which corroborated and illuminated this vision and which are also included in the book. For greater clarity, I will share a brief background of the situation in which these were received.

Since my conversion experience in 1971 I have had, at times, an ability to foresee certain future events accurately, but usually in a very general sense. I could also occasionally look at people and know details about them such as problems they were having or spiritual callings on their life. I understood this ability to be the Biblical gifts of "a word of knowledge" and "prophecy." Though I understood the usefulness of these gifts in ministry to people, I have not had much interest in the Biblical prophecies of end-time events, nor have I sought visions, revelations or understanding of them. I have actually been more oriented toward church history than I have impending events. I still remain ignorant of many of the popular end-time scenarios being projected and taught within the church.

After several years in the full time ministry I was convicted that I was shallow in my personal relationship to the Lord and therefore in my ministry as well. I felt like a real "Martha type," busy doing so many things for Him I had never really gotten to know Him. My lack of intimacy with the Lord had caused me to lean more on formulas and procedures than the anointing that is essential to giving life to truth. In 1980 I determined to leave the ministry until I had recovered "the simplicity of devotion to Christ." I was a pilot by trade so I took a job flying corporate aircraft, which gave me a lot of free time for study and prayer. I found a nice little church where I could sit on the back row and just enjoy the fellowship of the people. Except for teaching a few times I was not involved in ministry for the next seven years. Except for a very few occasions, I did not receive any prophetic "revelation" or operate in the gifts of the Spirit during that time.

In 1982 I received a specific call to return to the ministry; I also had a business opportunity open at the same time. Still feeling inadequate and shallow, and having just received the worse personal attack I had ever received from the enemy, I took the business opportunity. Though I did not fall into carnality or what might be considered overt sins, I certainly drifted from the Lord for the next five years as I became consumed in the business I was building. In 1987 I was again called back into ministry by the Lord with the word that my commission would be given to another if I did not return at that time. I did not really know what my "commission" was but I knew I did not want to lose it. I responded immediately to this call.

I was quite sure that I was not supposed to pastor again but I really did not know what I was going to do in ministry. I had not read a single Christian magazine or watched Christian television for over seven years and I had little knowledge of what was even going on in the church at large. I had written the book *There Were Two Trees In The Garden* a few years before and it had become quite popular, which had brought me a few invitations to speak. I called a few pastors that I knew or who had contacted me because of the book and let them know that I was available for ministry. After my first ministry trip in over seven years, I returned home feeling as empty and inadequate as ever, and quite out of step with the churches I had visited. The one encouragement that I had was feeling much closer to the Lord than I had for some time, and my desire to serve Him in ministry had returned.

The morning after I had returned home I went into my office to just catch up on some paperwork and to pray for insight on what I was to do in the ministry. After sitting down I felt an overwhelming presence of the Lord. Then, after seven years with no prophetic revelation, I had a three day prophetic experience in which I felt like the Lord tried to catch me up with all that I had missed! The present state of the church and the impending events that are contained in this book were almost all revealed during those three days.

## The Nature of the Revelations

Some of the revelation came in "open visions." These were visible, external visions that were like watching a cinema

9

screen. Others were gentle, internal visions that are like having the "eyes of your heart" opened. I now have frequent visions and dreams that are filled with symbolism requiring interpretation like most of the Biblical visions, but these were not that way; many of the details that you read in this book I actually saw in the visions.

Some of what is shared in this book did not come in vision form, but like a massive anointing with the gift of the word of knowledge—I just all of a sudden knew many details about future events just as though it had been poured into me. I do not know how to explain it any other way than I just would know things I had not known before. I was told that **"with the Lord one day is as a thousand years and a thousand years as one day"** (II Peter 3:8). He said that He could do in me in one day what He might take many years to do in another. I think that this in itself is a revelation of what is about to unfold. Many who now come into the kingdom will have to mature at a rate much faster than in the past because the time is now shorter.

I have always had a hunger for knowledge, reading at least a book per week throughout most of my adult life. Much of what I was drawn to reading was about church history or classical literature, but both my studies and interests would be random and scattered. Some of the understanding shared in this book came in literal conversation with the Lord. I did not hear His voice audibly but it was more intimate and real than I could ever remember knowing before. When the Lord spoke to me during this time His sentences were few and brief, but they would each give me keys to understanding much of the seemingly disconnected and unrelated knowledge I had accumulated over the years, but had never before been able to tie together.

Facts and events began to relate that I do not think I could have ever related together by myself. These keys of knowledge also gave me understanding of many Scriptures and current events that I have studied or encountered since then but was not familiar with at the time. The Lord said to me that He was restoring the years that the "locust had eaten." I honestly do not feel that I gained as much understanding during any other five years of my life as I did during those three days.

I usually relate the word "vision" to the prophetic event of seeing "pictures" either internally or externally. I consider "revelation" to be the receiving of knowledge or understanding that is beyond our natural ability to attain. Most of what is contained in this book was received either by vision or by revelation that was supernatural. Some of it is the result of my own studies, but even these were illuminated by an anointing so that I could see them in the perspective in which they are herein shared.

I often hear those who share visions or dreams saying that they do not understand them as if that somehow gives credibility to the experience. That has not been my experience. I perfectly understand what I am sharing here and would not share it if I did not understand it. I do confess that my eschatology was shallow because of my disinterest before I received this vision, and it probably still remains superficial by most people's standards. Some of the vague concepts of the future that I entertained were from a handful of books I had read during my early years as a Christian. Since this vision I have had more of an interest in eschatology, but of that which I have read or the people I have listened to, I confess that few have corroborated what I was shown. But neither have I heard any two that seem to corroborate each other!

Though much of the general knowledge I had accumulated had seemed disconnected before the vision experience, the way it all fit together after the vision gave me great confidence in what I was shown. Even so, I wanted to confirm my visions and understanding with the Scriptures, and I have. Of course, the Scriptures do not address many of the events of history or the end-time with much detail, but the pattern of what I see in the Bible very definitely confirms the pattern of what I have seen in this vision. I do not believe I would have understood many Scriptures the way I do now had I not received the vision.

## How the Vision Should Be Used

Of the few shallow concepts I had concerning eschatology, some were changed by this experience, and I believe changed in such a way as to more accurately comply with what the Scriptures teach. I do not believe in establishing doctrine with visions, dreams or prophetic revelation; these are given to help illuminate or illustrate the Scriptures, not establish new doctrines. Because of these visions many Scriptures were opened to me that I had never understood before.

Even so, I have only included a few Scriptural references here to leave room for the Lord to speak individually to those who read this, believing this will make it more meaningful and real to the reader. Just reading and agreeing with someone else's vision does not necessarily make it revelation to us. It is when the Lord confirms the word that we have our own encounter with Him and it is no longer just someone else's revelation. I believe we must always be like the men of

12

Samaria who came to believe in Jesus, not just because of the testimony of the woman at the well, but because they saw and heard Him for themselves.

## A Note on Prophecy

Since distributing the summary of the first vision, I have met others who have seen and recorded the same basic vision, in some cases with more clarity and detail. As we have been promised, **"Surely the Lord our God does nothing unless He reveals His secret counsel to His servants the prophets" [plural] (Amos 3:7)**. To be properly received, this vision must not be considered exclusive or all inclusive but one part that must be joined with others to give a complete picture.

The vision I was given ends during the harvest, at which point precisely I do not know. I am not sure how much more time remains after the events I have seen. I do know that it is time for judgment to begin, and it begins with the household of God (I Peter 4:17). The apostle explained, **"But when we are judged, we are disciplined by the Lord in order that we may not be condemned along with the world"** (I Corinthians 11:32). There is no safe place we can go, or anything we can do to escape the coming judgments, *except* to be found in Christ. Jesus is the Ark in Whom we find deliverance. If we are abiding in Him, we will be at the right place and doing the right thing. If there is a central theme that runs throughout this vision, it is that we must now return to our first love and never again be beguiled from the simplicity of devotion to Christ.

All things are to be summed up in Christ (Ephesians 1:10). As we abide in Him, we are fulfilling our purpose and calling in this hour, which is ultimately to bring every thought in

13

heaven and earth into obedience and harmony with Him. "All things were made through Him and for Him;" JESUS IS THE PURPOSE OF THE CREATION; He IS the plan of God. Jesus is the love, desire and delight of the Father. In all that was made, He was looking for His Son; He is looking for His Son in us.

There are a number of redundancies purposely included in this book. These are meant to recall attention to issues which are of the utmost importance. It is the nature and purpose of prophecy not to just foretell events but sometimes to provoke a response to the prediction which results in repentance and/or intercession which can change our destiny and the unfolding events. We see a number of Biblical examples of this, such as when Jonah preached in Nineveh. Even though Jonah did not preach a contingency that Nineveh's overthrow could be averted by repentance, it is implied in every prophecy of judgment.

## Our Destiny Can Be Changed

That Nineveh was not overthrown did not make Jonah a false prophet, but it was the fruit of a true and anointed prophetic word. How could such a heathen city possibly repent as it did with the preaching of one Jew, with no signs or miracles attesting to the word, without anointing? There are events contained in this prophecy which *can be changed* by repentance and intercession. There are also events which cannot and/or will not be changed because of their intricate place in the unfolding of the ultimate purpose of God. These are not revealed here because they were not revealed to me. I was just given the understanding that this was so. Our response should be prayer and repentance for all that He reveals today that we might be made into vessels fit for His use in effecting His purposes.

The sequence in which these events are laid out in this prophecy is not necessarily the sequence in which they will occur. Even in Biblical prophecy the sequence of events is often purposely jumbled so that it does not flow in the order in which it is to unfold. This was not done by the Lord to confuse us but to keep us dependent on Him for interpretation. This keeps us seeking Him and not just seeking understanding. The encounters we have with Him as He gives revelation and knowledge teach us His ways and not just facts. Because of this, we can preach His message by His Spirit and with His heart, rather than by the letter.

It is the nature of prophecy, both Biblical prophecy and that which comes by the New Covenant gift of prophecy, to be *general*. Again, prophecy is not given just to foretell impending events as much as it is given to prepare the church and invoke a response which will affect the events. If the Lord wanted to impress us with His ability to foretell He could have been far more specific in His own Biblical predictions; He could have given the names, dates and specifics of coming world leaders, nations, wars; instead of just saying that knowledge would increase, He could have foretold the inventing of aircraft, space travel, etc. Occasionally the Lord does get more specific in what He reveals, but usually He does not. He uses what He reveals to let us know where we need to seek Him for understanding. Again, it is in His purpose and for our best interest that He keeps us seeking Him for the important details, to fill in the blanks. **"It is the glory of God to conceal a matter, but the glory of kings is to search it out" (Proverbs 25:2).** The Lord uses prophecy to awaken searching hearts in His people. He has called us to rule in this life and it is the nature of godly kings to search out the mysteries and purposes of God.

I pray that as you seek understanding through this vision that you encounter Him, see His glory, and are changed by it in a way that would enable you to worship Him more perfectly in Spirit and truth. Only then can we properly understand His works.

Knowing that what I was shown during the series of visions and other "revelations" was still "seen through a glass darkly," and as I continually gain more understanding of the different aspects of this vision, I will add that information to each new printing. However, to maintain prophetic integrity, additions are added at the end of each section and dated. I am concerned with conveying what I have been entrusted with accurately, which may at times mean changing things I have previously misunderstood. So far I have not made any such changes but have only added further insight to a number of areas covered by this vision.

## The Reason for the Vision

Zechariah 8:9 sums up what I feel is the purpose of this vision: **"Thus says the Lord of hosts, 'Let your hands be strong, you who are listening in these days to these words from the mouth of the prophets, those who spoke in the day that the foundation of the house of the Lord of hosts was laid, to the end that the temple might be built.' "**

The church will have to be strong in the days to come, stronger than we are now. One word that I was given was that "The church in the West is almost completely unprepared for difficulty, and difficulties are coming."

We must learn to hear and properly respond to proven prophetic voices in the times ahead. Since the first part of this vision was given in 1987 I have witnessed a number of critical situations, even to the point of life and death, which depended on hearing and responding properly to words from those the Lord is establishing with trustworthy prophetic ministries.

The prophetic ministry is essential for the proper laying of the foundation of the House of the Lord (see Ephesians 2:20), which is essential if the temple (the church) is to be built. The restoration of prophetic ministry is not a goal, it is a means to a much higher goal—preparing a habitation for the Lord. If we lose sight of this ultimate purpose of the Lord, we will be misled by the lesser purposes.

# PART I

# *The Great Awakening*

*Chapter 1*

# The Harvest

**Jesus said, "The harvest is the end of the age"** (Matthew 13:39). Between now and the end of the age, more people will come to know Jesus than have from Pentecost until this time. Before the end, every village in every nation will have had the gospel preached to them. Every person living will hear His name. The knowledge of the Lord will cover the earth as the waters cover the sea, and many whole cities and some entire nations will be converted to Him. The magnitude of what is coming cannot be measured by anything that has ever happened before; even the cosmos itself will be electrified with its energy. More than a tithe of all the people who have ever lived, more than one billion souls, will call upon His name in true commitment resulting in true conversion.

This harvest will exceed every previous outpouring of the Spirit in one profound way—Jesus will be preached as Lord and not just Savior. During this harvest the gospel will change from "Come and be saved," to "Bow the knee, He is the King!" This is the seventh and last trumpet, or message, to be preached. This message will not come in word only, but in power and unprecedented demonstrations of the Spirit.

There is another aspect to the harvest that is the end of the age: the reaping of evil. A harvest is the reaping of everything that has been sown, both good and evil. The evil that was sown in man will also come to fruition during this time. While the "wheat" is being gathered, the "tares" will also be gathered into bundles or unified. However, the gathering of the tares is actually meant to aid the gathering of the wheat. The separation and distinction between the two seeds will become increasingly visible in the days to come. The "man of sin," or the personification of the "sin of man," will also be fully revealed and understood during the harvest. This is not to be feared; He who is in us is *much* greater than he who is in the world, and the least of those in the Kingdom of God has more power than all of the antichrists. Nevertheless, this evil must be understood or many will be unnecessarily captured by it.

## The Mobilization

This vision is given to encourage and prepare those who will be laborers in this great work. It includes certain ecclesiastical and world events which relate to this preparation. These are not shared for the purpose of emotional stimulation but because the information is needed for the church to accomplish her mandate. It is time to awaken, to be sober in spirit, and to give ourselves fully to the purposes for which we have been called. **"He died for all, that they who live** *should no longer live for themselves, but for Him…"* (II Corinthians 5:15). It is now time for us to walk in a manner worthy of our callings.

Every believer has a specific job to do; we have all been called for a purpose. The Lord wants every person whose name is written in His Book of Life to see his own name written, to know that he is known by Him, and to see clearly His plan for his life.

In the coming days, the most powerful army ever assembled will be mustered. This army will not be equipped with guns or swords, but no power in heaven or earth will prevail against it. Its leadership will seem undistinguished and in some cases invisible, but no human organization has ever equaled its discipline and resolve. This army has been enlisted by the Lord Himself; He will train it and He will lead it. When the battle unfolds, its members will march in perfect order, without deviating from their paths or crowding each other, unyielding in their resolve, with the least of them having more power than the greatest of their enemies. This is the army of God envisioned by the prophets, soon to be a reality.

To be numbered in this army will require a training and spiritual discipline exceeding the physical and mental discipline required of elite military units. In relation to this I was shown a war horse. This creature had been wild and easily frightened into spontaneous and uncontrolled reactions. After proper training he was able to charge into the face of canons, rifles and sabres, and yet never lost his composure. In the most deafening confusion of battle, he was able to feel and respond to the gentle nudge of his master's knee or heel, which directed him to turn or change his pace. This will be the discipline of the coming last day ministry. Regardless of the confusion and noise of the battle, the church will be so in touch with the Master that she will feel and respond to His most gentle nudging. Just as the war horse not trained properly would put himself and his rider in jeopardy, those who today do not submit to the Lord's discipline will be in grave danger in the coming days. ***"Today* if you hear His voice do not harden your heart"** (Hebrews 3:7-8).

## The Marvel of the Ages

The Lord has prepared a ministry for this last day which will be the marvel of men and angels. These will not be self-seeking or self-promoting, and most of them will remain unknown to the world and to much of the church. Their works and preaching will stir nations, but many will fade into the crowds and disappear before anyone even knows who they are.

Many of the most powerful apostles and prophets will remain nameless and faceless to the public. These have no desire to build major ministries and will not covet fame and fortune. They are "spiritual celibates;" they will not rape the bride. Just as a natural eunuch is given entirely to preparing the bride for the king, and has no desire for her as he is not even able to, these will be completely given to preparing the church for her King. Their whole purpose is to see the King's joy because they are truly His friends. These will follow Him wherever He goes.

While many of their peers have been seeking exposure and promotion for their ministries, these have been quietly preparing themselves just as Jesus did for His first thirty years. While others are advancing in ministry many of these have been retreating. While others have been building up, these have been digging down, trying to strengthen their foundations and deepen their roots. Though not in rebellion, and often grieving over it, these are usually out of harmony with much of the church. These are the ones about which it was said, **"We played the flute for you and you did not dance. We sang a dirge for you and you did not mourn"** (Matthew 11:17).

When the battle unfolds, much of the leadership in the church will have gained their positions through self-promotion and political manipulation. Many who are considered "generals" by the people will be privates in God's eyes. Some in the lower ranks in the people's eyes will be God's top generals. These will not even seek rank or position in the church at this time, but will quietly, sometimes incognito, direct the end-time strategy of the church. Their authority will be in their wisdom. Like Stephen, who was just a deacon but whose wisdom and power lit a fire that set a new course for

Christianity, this new breed, without fame or position, will direct some of the greatest events in history. Though men will never know many of them, the entire host of heaven and hell have known them from the beginning.

Not since Jesus has the enemy feared anyone like he does these selfless messengers of power. Just as he tried to destroy Moses and Jesus by killing the children, his present onslaught through abortion, drugs and disease is a desperate attempt to destroy these before they can mature.

Some of them will have been dragged through the dregs of human sin, trauma and despair before they are awakened. They will love much because they were forgiven of much and delivered of much. As deep as the enemy has been able to get his roots into them, that is how deep the Lord will fill them after their deliverance. Others will have been raised in religious shelter, but the good they know will be from the Tree of Knowledge and not the Tree of Life. Like Saul of Tarsus, these will struggle in religious anguish until their release; then they will be used to put the ax to the root of the tree that has caused all of the death from the beginning. These will shine with the light of the Tree of Life and bring healing to the nations.

## The Feet of the Body

The Lord began forming His "body" on the Day of Pentecost. Through the centuries He has continued building this body, adding to it those who overcame in every age. The last members to be added to this body are metaphorically referred to as the "feet." Just as our feet touch the earth while the rest of the body stands erect in the air, the "feet" of the Lord's body will touch the earth but represent the entire body that stands completed in the heavenlies. The Scriptures say that all of His enemies will be crushed under His *feet*. Even so, these are not acting alone but are merely fulfilling and accomplishing that which was prepared by all of those who went before them.

When Jesus was asked about the authority by which He did the works, He responded with a question for them: **"Was the baptism of John of God or of men?"** This was not an arbitrary question; the answer to this question was the answer to their question. Jesus had credentials exceeding those of anyone who had ever walked this earth. From the first prophecy given to the woman about her Seed who would crush the serpent through an unending chain of prophets and righteous men, including all of the ritual of their own Law, every word had pointed to Him. John stood as the representative of that order who had prepared His way and testified that He was indeed the Lamb of God. To be baptized by John was to acknowledge this testimony of the One who was *born* king.

The "feet" of the body of Christ will carry the credentials for all of those who have gone before them. They will be joined to each other like no other body of people have ever been joined, but they will also be joined to the true believers of all ages who lived and prophesied of this day. As Jesus promised, the things that He did, and even greater things, will be done in His name because He went to the Father. His faithful will soon walk in unprecedented power and authority. In the near future the church will not be looking back at the first century church with envy because of the great exploits of those days, but all will be saying that He certainly did save His best wine for last. The most glorious times in all of history have now come upon us. You who have dreamed of one day being able to talk with Peter, John and Paul are going to be surprised to find that they have all been waiting to talk to you! You have been chosen to see the harvest, the fruit of the seeds that they were planting.

We have come to the most blessed time to walk with God, but we must not be arrogant. The feet would not be of any use without the rest of the body, and we would not be where we are except for those who laid down their lives before us. When the feet are joined to the rest of the body, the whole body will be rejoicing in the triumph of this day and receiving of its fruit.

*Chapter 2*

# Preparing
# for the Harvest

The nature of spiritual truth can be found in Ecclesiastes 3:1, "There is an appointed time for everything…" There is a time to plant and a time to reap, but there will not be a reaping if we have missed the time to plant. The church has had a "reaping mentality" which has caused it to overlook many of the planting seasons. Because of this our harvests have amounted to little more than the gathering of what has grown wild.

Many have not been willing to work unless they could count what they accomplished, to put it in reports, newsletters and books. We like to see immediate results or often we feel like failures. Indeed, many missionaries would lose their support if they did not produce quick results. Only eternity will tell how much this has cost the church in her effectiveness. The Lord will soon change this mentality in His laborers. Just as the farmer does not plant the seed and then stand there waiting for fruit, these will have the wisdom to plant knowing that the results of this labor may not be seen for a long time and may not be seen by them at all. Some will plant, others will water, but God will give and receive the increase.

Even science verifies the Lord's statement that a seed cannot sprout unless it first dies or goes through a dormant period. God created this protective mechanism in the seed that keeps it from sprouting until conditions are right for growth. In order for it to sprout, a seed must have the proper amount of water, heat and light. Having two out of three of these will not work. This is to keep the seed from being fooled into thinking it is spring because of a wet warming trend. If these are not accompanied with enough light each day, the seed knows that spring has not really come.

The same is true of spiritual seeds. We may want to see immediate results from our preaching or witnessing, but the Lord will protect the seeds until the conditions are right for growth. Metaphorically, spiritual seeds require the same basic conditions as natural seeds: water, heat and light. Water speaks of the Word of God, of which there must be an abundance. Heat speaks of circumstances; most have to be in the fire of trials before they will turn to the Lord. Light speaks of Divine revelation which enables us to realize that it is God who is speaking through the Word and circumstances.

Between each great move of God there is a period of quietness in which there appears to be little happening. This is the time for planting. As stated, our "reaping mentality" has caused us to miss many of these planting seasons, but a new strategy and a zeal for sowing seeds is about to sweep the church. Those seeking to plant for the harvest will be given words of wisdom and words of knowledge for this purpose. Most of these will be subtle, gently arousing questions in those to whom they are given. Others will astonish and profoundly move the recipients. At the proper time both will accomplish their purpose.

## Using Revelation Gifts

To be effective, the "revelation gifts" must be used in the wisdom of the Holy Spirit. If we had received a word of knowledge about the woman at the well, how many of us would have jumped up and called her an adulteress? Jesus did not. He gently led her in the conversation and never did rebuke her for her sins. The reality of Who she had encountered more than likely convicted her of the adultery and every other sin.

There are times for bold confrontations, such as the Lord had with the Pharisees, but that could have been devastating for this particular woman, or even for Nicodemas, who was himself a Pharisee. One of the least emphasized but most important gifts of the Spirit is the gift of a word of wisdom. This is the supernatural impartation of the mind of Christ into specific situations. This gift is often a more subtle and less spectacular gift than the word of knowledge or the power gifts, but without it the others may be rendered less effective, or even counterproductive in accomplishing God's purposes.

The preaching of Jesus must be in obedience to the Holy Spirit who was given to testify of Him. The Lord has blessed and used many different strategies and tactics devised by zealous men in the past to reach the lost, but this will not be the case in the future. Great trials and testings will come upon the church until His laborers are utterly submitted to the moving of the Spirit. This will multiply the effectiveness of His messengers and enable Him to trust them with power and authority never before given to men.

The industrial age disease which requires us to have a formula for everything, which demanded the packaging of the gospel into spiritual laws, is contrary to true evangelism. Our formulas will get a "decision" out of a few, and may actually result in the conversion of some, but often the effect of this type of witness is to inoculate the masses so that they are immune to the true witness, which is a regenerating encounter with God. The laborers who are coming will be armed with far more than a recipe for getting a quick decision. **"For the kingdom of God does not consist in words but in power"**

(I Corinthians 4:20), and power is about to come upon the true witnesses after they have been trained.

This is not meant to belittle the efforts of any ministry seeking to bring people into a relationship with Jesus, but we will not be prepared for what is coming if we do not recognize our present condition. Immaturity does have its place. It is acceptable for a one year old to wear diapers. It is a reflection of her immaturity, but a one year old is supposed to be immature. In fact, she may even be quite mature for her age. But if she were twelve and still had to wear diapers there would be a problem! Many ministries and churches are quite immature, but they are young. The issue is—are we growing up? The events in the days ahead will demand our maturity.

## The Ingathering

The magnitude of this harvest will ultimately astonish even the most optimistic believers. Congregations of less than a hundred will be adding a thousand believers a week for periods of time. Meetings which begin spontaneously will stir entire cities, continuing until they fill the largest stadiums night after night. Previously popular sports events will be abandoned in many regions for lack of interest. Whole towns, with populations of thousands, will swarm upon neighboring towns to evangelize them. The news media will be dominated by the harvest until they have fanned the flames throughout the world. News teams will follow apostles like national leaders, recording great miracles which will be shown with unabashed enthusiasm. Some of these individual broadcasts will result in more conversions than Christian networks have seen during their entire existence. This is not a negative reflection about the work Christian networks have accomplished, but a reflection of the magnitude of what is coming.

Large cities will experience periods of "zero crime" as their populations come under the conviction of the Holy

Spirit, and the light of the church drives darkness from entire regions. Pornography, prostitution, illegal drugs, abortion and drunkenness will cease to exist in many areas without the passage of a single law. Large factories and businesses will shut down for days at a time so their employees can attend special meetings. Whole nations will give themselves to periods of prayer and fasting. The inflow of new believers will be so great in places that relatively new believers will find themselves leading large congregations. Some churches will be dividing every few months, not because of conflicts, but because their growth is so great they must keep the size down to what is manageable, with each split resulting in the birth of new congregations.

The Lord will continually be on the minds of the people. Coffee breaks, lunch breaks and siestas will become Bible studies and prayer meetings. Cities will sponsor bonfires for burning pornography, witchcraft and astrological parapher-nalia and illegal drugs. Warlocks, witches, mediums and even mafia chieftains will be bowing the knee to Jesus and entering into salvation with great joy. Street gangs will be sending Bibles and gifts to one another and prisons will become churches which will give the Body of Christ some of its greatest teachers.

Miracles which exceed even some of the most spectacular Biblical marvels will cause whole nations to acknowledge Jesus. Leaders of some of the most powerful communist countries will be openly confessing the Lord and exhorting their people to follow Him. The visible glory of the Lord will appear upon some for periods of time and this glory will heal everyone it touches. The pillar of fire that led Israel will not even compare to the intense presence of the Lord in these days. The appearances of angels will be so common that they will cease to be related as significant events. The Lord Him-self will appear to councils of apostles and elders to give them directives. This will impart a courage and peace which will astonish and gain the respect of even the most vehement opposers. Never has the Lord been as personal and intimate with His people as He will be in these days. Believers will be in awe continually, wondering each day what great new things they will see.

One of the most extraordinary characteristics of the harvest will be the youthfulness of the laborers. Teenagers will be the backbone of the revival, and preteens will be some of its greatest evangelists. Young children will cast out demons, heal the sick, raise the dead, and divert raging floods with a word. Some will actually take dominion over entire hospitals and mental institutions, healing every patient in them by laying hands on the buildings. During the harvest the world will understand that "... **the children whom the Lord has given me are for signs and wonders**..." (Isaiah 8:18).

## The Darkness

As the light of the gospel is shining so brightly, much of the world will be in its deepest darkness. There will be regions where the peace and love of the Lord reign, and these will become fortresses from which the church will go out and attack the fear and paranoia sweeping the rest of the earth.

There will be great defeats following victories, and great victories following defeats. Large cities will be under almost the complete dominion of the Lord. Others will be almost completely in the grip of an evil more terrible than we may presently be able to comprehend. The Lord will never have moved in such great power, but neither will the enemy have ever been so desperate. At the end of the vision both light and darkness are increasing throughout the entire earth.

We must be prepared for this conflict. There will be martyrs during the harvest. In places, the church will be almost completely wiped out. But the lives of these martyrs will be seed for a harvest in that same place. The places where the enemy makes his most powerful attacks are the very places where the greatest advances of the gospel will be made. Remember that light shines into darkness—it is not the other way around. When you open your shades at night, darkness does not come in; light shines out. Light is more powerful than darkness and will always overcome it.

## The Fishnet

For the coming harvest the Lord is preparing a great spiritual "fishnet" which will be able to hold the catch that is coming. This net is formed by the linking together of His people. The strength of this net will be determined by the strength of the interrelationships and intercommunication of His people. The stronger the intercommunication and inter-relationships, the stronger this net will be. This is not only happening in the local churches among members but between ministries, congregations and the different streams in the Body of Christ throughout cities, states, and crossing international barriers around the world.

Ephesians 4:15-16 states: "… **We are to grow up in all aspects into Him, who is the Head, even Christ, from whom the whole body, being fitted and held together by that which every *joint* supplies.**" A joint is not a part, but it is where two parts come together. There is a great fitting together going on in the Spirit now, and it will increase on all levels. With each new joint there will be substantial growth and edification for those who are joined.

The Spirit is compelling pastors to get together with other pastors, prophets with prophets, apostles with apostles, and even whole congregations are beginning to visit and interrelate with other congregations apart from their own circles of emphasis. This is the Lord's doing. Some of these meetings may seem fruitless because of improper agendas, but they will bear fruit; there will be links made. Soon the Lord's presence in these meetings will melt all presumption and the facades which separate us from union with Him and each other. His presence will stimulate a worship that brings about Psalm 133 unity; as we anoint the Head with our worship, the oil will flow down to the edge of His robes until it covers the entire body.

The Lord is beginning this breakdown of barriers with the leadership because this is where most originate and where they are the strongest. As the walls come down here the entire body will begin flowing together. If the leaders resist this move the Lord will continue it through the congregations. These will begin to relate to other members of the body of Christ and their bonds will grow stronger regardless of the opposition from resistant pastors. This is a move of the Holy Spirit that cannot be stopped. The pastors and leaders who continue to resist this tide of unity will be removed from their place.

Some who are presently in leadership that resist this move will become so hardened they will become opposers and persecutors of those who are accomplishing the Lord's purposes. Others will be changed and will repent of their hardness of heart even though, in some cases, their resistance to the Holy Spirit will have disqualified them from leadership. This growing tide of unity in the church will ultimately reveal the true nature of everyone in spiritual leadership. Those who have been building for themselves and their own reputations will be threatened by this move because it is beyond their control. Those with a "control spirit" will continually be the greatest threat to the true moves of God. Those who have been truly ordained by God, and not just an institution, will become increasingly determined to give up "control" over their people and circumstances, deferring to the Holy Spirit. The "control" they relinquish will be replaced by a spiritual authority grounded in the peace and rest of God. What is coming is beyond any man's ability to control. Only the Holy Spirit can order this work, and He is now starting to take His authority. *Those with a "control spirit" will be the greatest opposers of every move of God until the end.*

Because of the magnitude of the "catch," this net will be rent many times and will be in need of constant mending. Much of the discord now taking place in the church is used by the Lord to prepare those whose task in the harvest will be almost exclusively devoted to the mending and binding of this great net. These peacemakers will have a great part in building this net and will have a major impact on the effectiveness of the entire revival.

Those that seem to always find themselves in the middle of conflicts should be encouraged with the knowledge that they are being prepared for a great work. Even with the awesome presence of the Lord there will still be bickering and disputing among the disciples, just as there was among the twelve. Even great apostles like Paul and Barnabas allowed issues to divide them, and it will happen at times with even the greatest men of God. But the net will get mended and will become even stronger where it was broken.

Some who were greatly used of God in the past have become too rigid in doctrinal emphasis or are too entangled with spiritual "Ishmaels" to participate in this revival. Some of these will try to join the work, but their interrelationships will be so superficial that they will quickly be torn from the net by the first catch. Those who are linked together by doctrine or who gather around personalities will quickly be torn away. Only those who are joined by and through Jesus alone will stand the pressure this harvest will bring upon the church (Colossians 1:17).

The redemption of so many will bring much joy to the church but these new converts will come with problems which will bring enormous stress to congregations and ministers. The cords of unity must be very strong to withstand this pressure. Those who have not learned to take the Lord's yoke, instead of carrying the burdens themselves, will be overwhelmed. Entering the Sabbath rest of the Lord will become a major emphasis in preparation for the harvest. We must heed this word!

## True Conversions

A large number who are now considered Christians have never been led to the Lord. They were led to the church, to a personality, or to a doctrine or emphasis. Some of these will think they are important links in the net but will actually become part of the harvest, starting over again on the proper Foundation—a relationship with Jesus. This will include a number of well known ministers and pastors. Their humility in this will lead multitudes to question and strengthen their own relationships to the Lord. This will do much to undergird and encourage the entire body of Christ.

Denominations, extra-local fellowships and circles of emphasis will begin disbanding and severing their ties, even those that were ordained by God for a season, in order to be a part of this great net. For some these ties will just be ignored or forgotten until they have passed away, almost without notice, because of the greater intensity and substance of this new move. For others it will be a very painful rending as they are persecuted and rejected by those who do not understand. The pain of these broken relationships will not last long for those who must endure them; a true church life that has been the desire of Christians since Pentecost will soon be realized by those who have not lost their hope.

Some leaders will actually disband their organizations as they realize they are no longer relevant to what God is doing. Others will just leave them behind to disband themselves. Ultimately, all circles of ministry or influence with individual identities will dissolve into a single identity of simply being

Christians for all who become part of this harvest. The present streams and movements will eventually flow into the one River of Life. When this happens there will be nothing left that can stop or even hinder the force with which it flows. It will sweep about like a great flood that carries away everything in its path. Every religious fortress and lie which exalts itself against the knowledge of God will be swept away by this great river. As the different streams of light begin flowing together, their power will become concentrated like the greatest laser from which there is no protection. The cloak behind which every religious impostor hides will be stripped away so that they are apparent to all. This light will ultimately become too bright for any darkness to hide within the church.

Single presbyteries will form over cities and localities. These will be made up of pastors and leaders from many different denominations, movements and independent churches. Their unity in purpose, as well as that of the various congregations, will be a marvel to the world that is itself degenerating into chaos and paranoia.

As Paul wrote to the Corinthians: **"I thank my God always concerning you, for the grace of God which was given you in Christ Jesus, that in everything you were enriched in Him, in all speech and all knowledge, even as the testimony of Christ was confirmed in you so that you are not lacking in *any* gift, awaiting eagerly the revelation of our Lord Jesus Christ..."** (I Corinthians 1:4-7). The church at the end of the age will have this same testimony of Christ confirmed in her, not lacking in any gift as she waits eagerly for the revelations of our Lord Jesus.

## Chapter 3

# The Travail
# of the Spirit

When declaring events that would signal the end of the age, the Lord noted that these were **"the beginning of birth pangs"** (Matthew 24:8). The harvest and accompanying events will unfold just as travail comes upon a woman in labor. That is, the contractions begin suddenly but at first are infrequent and relatively light. The closer the process comes to the birth, the more intense and the more frequent the contractions become.

The first contractions signaling the end of the age actually occurred several hundred years ago with the beginning of the Reformation. Over two hundred years passed before there was another, then a hundred years, until now the time between these spiritual contractions is only decades. Soon it will be just years between them with each one becoming significantly more intense. We are getting closer to the birth of the Day of the Lord.

In labor, the contractions actually push the baby into the birth canal, while opening the cervix to allow entry into the world. Likewise, with each spiritual contraction, that which the Lord was bringing to birth was pushed further down the canal, and the way was opened a little wider for its eventual manifestation.

During childbirth the mother can complicate and endanger herself and the emerging child because *her natural tendencies are to do the opposite of what she should be doing to aid the process.* This is why education through "natural" childbirth classes has enabled mothers to give birth with much less pain. They teach the mother how to resist her tendencies and do what will actually help the process. If the church is to flow with the birth process we too must resist some of our natural tendencies.

During the "transition" stage when the baby is entering the birth canal, the mother usually goes through severe disorientation. Physicians specializing in natural childbirth have found that it helps for the mother to have a "focal point" on which to concentrate during this time. It is also essential for the mother to heed the instructions of the labor "coach" (usually the husband) and to obey them regardless of her pain or feelings.

The Lord used "birth pangs" to describe the unfolding of these times because it is an appropriate metaphor. Unfortunately, the church, being in much ignorance of the actual process through which she is going, has often continued to follow her natural instincts instead of the voice of the Lord. This has caused her to strive counterproductively through much of the process, leaving her now weary and expended as we enter the most critical stages of delivery. It has never been more critical for the church to concentrate with discipline and determination upon her "focal point," the ultimate purpose of God, that she might bring many new sons to birth. She must become obedient to the instructions of her husband, Jesus. If we don't, we can bring grave complications upon ourselves.

## The Restoration of Ministries

Beginning with Luther, each spiritual contraction resulted in a major, basic Christian truth being restored to the church, as well as one of the five ministries given for the equipping of the saints, as listed in Ephesians, chapter four. During the Middle Ages apostles, prophets, evangelists, pastors and teachers were unrecognized and had generally ceased to function in the church except in isolated and rare occasions. The church was for over a thousand years dominated by a priestcraft, but with the restoration of truth to the church there also had to come a restoration of true ministry.

With the beginning of the Reformation, the PASTOR was restored to recognized ministry. Over two hundred years later, with the Wesleys, the EVANGELIST was restored and attained general recognition and acceptance. The Pentecostal and Latter Rain revivals began the restoration of the gifts of the Holy Spirit, but it was not until the Charismatic and Third Wave Renewals that the TEACHING ministry was fully restored. Teaching was the primary emphasis and a much greater anointing came upon this ministry during these movements. Until that time most of those with a teaching ministry were relegated to seminaries or seminars. Now this ministry is truly being incorporated into the life of the local church, resulting in the building up of the whole body.

The next spiritual contraction will bring about the restoration and recognition of the PROPHETS. We will see the prophetic ministry become the primary focus of attention during the next few years as a much greater anointing comes upon this ministry than has been seen since Biblical times. Just as there were some pastors, evangelists and teachers in the Body of Christ before their ministries were fully restored, there have been some prophets in the church; they just have not received the understanding, anointing, and acceptance that they soon will.

The church has been well prepared for the restoration of this ministry. The Body of Christ is now aware that it must have a much greater clarity of vision and revelation of the

Divine purpose in the days to come. The prophet is **"the eye of the body"** (see Isaiah 29:10); and when the eye is single or unified, the whole body will be full of light. We are promised this unity of vision in Isaiah 52:8: **"Listen! Your** *watchmen* **lift up their voices, they will shout joyfully** *together* **[in unity]; for they will see eye to eye when the Lord restores Zion."** Those who are emerging with a true prophetic mantle will be joined in a union that is unprecented in this ministry.

## The Two Enemies of Every Movement

The Charismatic movement was sidetracked and stifled by well-meaning but misguided men who sought to bring order and unity through human initiatives, organizations and control. *The same will be true with the restoration of the prophetic ministry.* Misguided leaders will ultimately bring as much confusion and disorientation as was afflicted upon previous renewals. We must understand that every time the Lord plants wheat the enemy is going to come and plant tares. The primary diversion that the enemy will use in order to sidetrack every new move of God will be the "control spirit" and the "political spirit."

As lawlessness increases, many church leaders will be prone to overreact to it in trying to bring order. These over-reactions that use human strength, control and methods will ultimately result in even more disorder and confusion. The control spirit seeks to get Christian leaders to overstep their authority and try to do the work of the Holy Spirit in the lives of others. The political spirit simply tries to get Christian leaders to submit more to the pressures of the people, or even their enemies, than they do the Lord. These two demonic powers usually work together, causing the subjected leaders to sometimes appear overly accommodating and at other times harsh and intransigent. In this way they are able to knock a movement off course in a number of directions at once.

Even so, we must not disregard the wheat just because tares have been sown in the midst of it. We must glean the good seed from every movement regardless of how far it gets knocked off track. The church will need the contributions of each movement to fulfill her last day mandate. Some of the movements that suffered the greatest attack of the collaborating demons of control and politics were those who originally had some of the most important truths. In time, the tares in every movement will be gathered into recognizable "bundles" to be cast into the fire, but we must not forget the wheat that has come from them.

## False Prophets and False Teachers

We must understand that one may be a false teacher or prophet *and still be a born again brother in the Lord*! The Lord Jesus Himself warned of this when He said, **"For many will come in My name, saying, 'I am the Christ,' and will mislead many"** (Matthew 24:5). Some have interpreted this as indicating that these would come saying that *they* were the Christ, but that is not what He said. He said that they would come saying He, Jesus, was indeed the Christ, but they would still be deceivers. One becomes a false teacher or prophet when he tries to walk in a ministry to which he has not been ordained by God. This does not mean that they are not redeemed believers; they are just deceived into presuming commission to a ministry to which God has not called them.

The Lord went on to say that there would be false Christs and false prophets who would arise and show great signs and wonders in an attempt to mislead even the elect (i.e. true prophets or teachers). There will be tares sown among the wheat, but there would be no counterfeit if that which is true did not also exist. There would be no counterfeit money if there was not true money. The only reason the enemy brings false signs and wonders is because there are real signs and wonders.

## Distinguishing the True From the False

The Lord has told us how we may distinguish the false from the real in John 7:18, **"He who speaks from himself seeks his own glory [literally "recognition"]; but he who is seeking the glory of the One who sent him, he is true and there is no unrighteousness in him."** Regardless of how tearfully one uses the name of Jesus, self-seeking and self-promotion will always surface in those who are self-appointed. Regardless of how much one talks of giving all the glory to God, those who are seeking their own recognition are speaking from themselves, at best.

Some of the most destructive false prophets will be those who were called as true prophets but have let self-seeking gain entrance into their ministries. These may be gifted with the true spiritual gifts. **"The gifts and callings of God are irrevocable"** (Romans 11:29). The Lord does not take back His gifts even when we become unfaithful. He remains faithful even when we do not. That is why so many effective ministries have fallen into immorality, drunkenness and other forms of corruption, but the gifts would continue to function in their ministry. That is why the Lord told us to judge by fruit, not gifts.

Gifts are given, but fruit must be grown. The decade of the eighties should have awakened us to this important fact. Unfortunately many will not heed this warning. Paul marveled at how the Corinthians could **"...bear with anyone if he enslaves you, if he devours you, if he takes advantage of you, if he exalts himself, if he hits you in the face"** (II Corinthians 11:20). Carnal men will always respond more readily to carnal strength because the natural man does not understand the ways of the Spirit. The church will continue to be misled and humiliated until she learns not to follow after carnal strength and mere human leadership.

Even with all of its problems, the spiritual contraction bringing the restoration of the prophetic ministry to the church will be so great that many will believe it is in fact the harvest. Multitudes will be streaming to the Lord as this will be one of the greatest revivals in history. These millions who come in are not the harvest but are called as laborers for the true harvest that is yet to come. But these multitudes must not just be herded into "sheep pens," but they must be thoroughly equipped for service in the harvest that is yet to come.

## The Second Move

There will be another, even greater move, of the Holy Spirit, or spiritual contraction, following the next one. During this second move a true APOSTOLIC authority will be restored and recognized within the advancing church. The ministry that opened the church age will also be the ministry that closes it.

It is noteworthy that these ministries are being restored in the reverse order in which they were lost to the church. The early church began in a place of light and regressed into darkness. The last day church is coming out of the darkness and progressing toward increasing light. This light will increase until the fullness of day comes with the full revelation of Jesus.

As stated, all of these ministries have existed in the church before their restoration in part but, with the contraction that restored their recognition, came a commission restoring a greater anointing and authority. Just as there were evangelists before Wesley and teachers before the Charismatic and Third Wave Renewals, there are some true prophets and apostles in the church today. But even the most significant of these are not yet walking in the full authority of their offices, but they will be.

The prophets soon to be commissioned will greatly exceed in gifts and authority that which is presently accepted as prophetic ministry and ultimately that which has even historically existed. The glory of the latter house will be greater than that of the former. This is not to imply that the house is greater. In fact, the latter house (temple) was inferior to the former, but the glory to be revealed in it was greater. That a greater glory is coming upon the last day house has nothing to do with the righteousness or worthiness of either the early church or the last day church, but is entirely related to the purpose of God for the times.

A power and authority is about to be given to some which will exceed all precedents. This is to fulfill the Lord's promise that even greater works than His would be performed. Those who walk in this will not be perfect men; they will make mistakes just as their Biblical counterparts did. A number of these will demonstrate unprecedented revelation and power. There will be many others, like the companies of prophets who attended Samuel and Elijah, who will seem average by comparison but who at times will accomplish the most extraordinary individual exploits. Some of these will spend their entire lives preparing to give just one word to the church or to a nation, with that one word accomplishing as much as others have in a lifetime of service.

The advancing church has gone from the Protestant gospel, to the Evangelical, to the Pentecostal, to the Charismatic. Each move felt they had the "full gospel," but none did—*and neither will the next move.* Our understanding of even the most basic doctrines is about to expand dramatically, but it will still fall short of the apostolic faith. This will not be fully restored until the apostolic ministry has been fully restored.

With the restoration of the prophetic ministry, a vision of the apostolic faith will be imparted.

## We Are in Labor Until Christ Is Formed

Even with all of the problems, shallowness and even deceptions and false doctrines, great truths were restored to the church through every previous Renewal. Many of these truths were carried to extremes and error because the church allowed them to become the focal point in place of the only One upon Whom we must keep our attention. This has led to almost every disorientation, and it will every time we allow it to happen.

The Way is not a principle or formula but a Person. Walking in Truth is not just assimilating and agreeing with certain spiritual facts, but it is following a Person. Deception is not just misunderstanding doctrines or principles; *deception is not being in God's will*. We can know all truth accurately and still be disobedient. Our goal is more than just knowing the book of the Lord; it is knowing the Lord of the book. We can memorize the Bible but not know the Word Himself. Jesus is Truth, and He is the summation of all the individual truths that were restored or will be restored in the coming move. We must never again allow ourselves to be distracted from the simplicity of devotion to Christ Himself.

Unfortunately, many will once again lose the focal point and give their whole attention to new truths and emphases. New "streams" with great new truths and dynamic ministries will add much life to the church, but some of them will result in great disorientation just as many previous renewal movements did. Some who were fooled and distracted during the previous moves of the Holy Spirit will not be fooled again but will be used to give strength and stability during this time, keeping many on track and out of confusing diversions.

When true apostolic authority is commissioned, it will signal the end of the transition stage of our travail. Then the final stage, which results in the birth of the end-time ministry, will commence. In natural childbirth it is during this stage that a remarkable clarity of purpose and strength return to the mother, which even in "natural" childbirth seems supernatural. This is the time to push until the child comes forth. The restored apostolic faith will so energize the church with resolve that the pains will be forgotten. The reason for centuries of travail and six millenniums of sacrifice and hope will then be seen with our own eyes.

With the restoration of apostolic ministry, the diverse vision of the church will then be concentrated upon the Lord Jesus Himself. All things are to be summed up in Him as He IS the complete Purpose of God. The depths of the wisdom and knowledge of God that are found in Him will be revealed, and all eyes will be turned upon His glory. Just as light concentrated becomes awesome power in the laser, the focus of our attention upon the Lord Himself will result in the power being released in the church to accomplish her end-time mandate. At this time, all true seekers who were distracted from the River of Life by the little tributaries which feed it will return to that River never to be distracted again. The Head will finally be joined to the body. Then we will worship in Spirit and Truth.

## They Will Each March in Line

For nearly two thousand years the Son of Man has been seeking a place to lay His head, a place where He can be the Head. A primary function of the apostolic ministry is the restoration of Jesus as the Head of His church. As this becomes a reality, the church will become the greatest demonstration of order and harmony ever witnessed in human affairs. Like the most disciplined and athletic human body, the level of cooperation between ministries, churches and every individual who serves His name will be the marvel of the world, which confounds the greatest thinkers of the day. Without human organization, the flow and interchange of ministry will be breathtaking in its precision.

When an evangelist or apostle plants in an area, others will appear with perfect timing to water those seeds. Seeds will not get planted which do not get watered; and seeds will not be watered that have not been planted. There will be increasing interchange and fellowship between ministries, but directives and strategy will not come from mere human planning or computer systems, but by the Holy Spirit. The prophetic word will be flowing with purity and accuracy unsurpassed in church history. Major conferences of the apostles and elders will be convened with no invitations being issued, and no word being passed concerning it. The Holy Spirit will speak to each who is to attend and He will preside. The Lord Himself will be directing the harvest of the world like the most perfectly managed farm.

The Lord's direction of His work will include even the smallest details. When His teams need capital, food, or other resources, they will not even have to ask before it is provided. When Bibles or other materials are needed, they will arrive. When a body of believers needs instruction, the right teacher will be passing through right on time. There is no computer system or organization known to man that can match the efficiency and timing with which the Lord will direct the harvest. This will all be even more remarkable because of the increasing chaos into which the world will be degenerating during this time.

The preparation for this great emphasis of the Spirit will be knowing the Lord's voice. The discipline of the Spirit upon those who are being prepared for this last day ministry will be most severe. The consequences of being insensitive to the

Spirit in our affairs will become increasingly dramatic and immediate. Christians will find themselves no longer able to get away with the casual manner in which they have previously walked and lived. Presumption that seemed to have little or no effect on us in the past will soon bring quick and sobering discipline or retribution.

As the hand of the Lord becomes obvious in the direction of His ministry teams, some missionary societies and ministries will begin disbanding their own planning organizations to become completely dependent on the Holy Spirit's guidance. Some organizations will remain and will be used in the disbursing of information and the teaching and assisting of interchange throughout the church, but direction and guidance will increasingly become the domain of the Holy Spirit alone.

## There Is a Time for Everything

Like the manner in which birth pangs come upon a woman, there will be times of great intensity and advancement in the church followed by periods of rest. There will be times of upheaval in the world followed by times of relative peace. There will be different timing for different places. One city may be experiencing great revival while another is not. When the Spirit is poured out on the second, the first may be quiet. There will be great persecution upon the church in one part of the world while others will be enjoying peace and favor. Because of this it is even more critical that every church and every individual know the Lord's voice and be able to hear Him for themselves.

There are some general patterns that the whole church and the whole earth will be moving towards, though at different paces. The church will be increasing in light and power; the world will be sinking into unprecedented darkness. As the true church grows in faith and clarity of vision, the earth will be swept with wave after wave of paranoia.

This will increase until no government on earth will be able to control its people. Mobs, sometimes numbering hundreds of thousands, will be sweeping about destroying everything in their path. Plagues, natural disasters and conflicts will bring about such loss of life that it will be nearly impossible to bury all of the dead. Men will be desperately seeking anyone to take authority over them for their protection, but no one will be willing. The remaining governments will be little more than gangs who have banded together to protect their own interests or to plunder the weak.

The vision ended with increasing darkness and destruction in the world, and increasing glory and harvest in the church. I do not feel that it would be profitable for me to speculate about what takes place after this or to impose my own doctrinal understandings of following events. Soon the prophetic vision of the church will increase dramatically. Those who are obedient seekers of the Lord and His purposes will not be surprised or overcome by events or circumstances.

## Chapter 4

# Equipping the Saints

A great task lies ahead for the entire church. We have much to do to prepare ourselves for what is coming. As wonderful as it will be to witness the harvest, it will bring enormous stress upon the church. The Lord wants every new convert properly cared for and equipped for their own purpose. This will be impossible without the grace and strength of the Lord, but we must also understand that those He has called to responsibility will give an account. The Lord will not continue to tolerate ministries or churches that do not properly equip their people.

Every believer is called to ministry, and every single one is needed. It is imperative that each believer find his proper place in the body, begin to function in it, and be able to teach others to do the same. Our commission is to:

**Go therefore and MAKE DISCIPLES [not just converts] of ALL NATIONS [not just individuals], baptizing them in the name of the Father and the Son and the Holy Spirit, teaching them to observe ALL that I commanded you (Matthew 28:19-20).**

Making disciples is our mandate. The Lord is now enlisting those who will lay aside every encumbrance and the entanglements of everyday affairs to do all things for the sake of His gospel. One of the most important things that we can do for the sake of the gospel is to prepare others to do what we do, and when possible, to do it better than we can do it and to advance beyond our own limits when possible. One of the primary vehicles for the equipping of the saints will be the institution of home groups as a foundational structure of the church. Here many of the church's most effective ministers will be identified and raised up.

## The Purpose of the Ministry

Those in positions of leadership who are just feeding themselves, and not properly preparing the saints for their service, will soon be severely disciplined or removed from their place. The church does not exist to provide for the ministry; the ministry exists to provide for the church. One of the most frequently preached Scriptures over the last few decades is Ephesians 4:11-12: **"He gave some as apostles, and some as prophets, and some as evangelists, and some as pastors and teachers, FOR THE EQUIPPING OF THE SAINTS FOR THE WORK OF SERVICE,"** yet almost nowhere has this been accomplished.

There are some congregations that are preparing some of the people for some parts of the ministry, but the Lord wants all of His people equipped. Paul declared to the Corinthian church that **"the testimony of Christ was *confirmed* in you so that you were not lacking in ANY gift"** (I Corinthians 1:6-7). Jesus manifested all of the gifts of the Holy Spirit and all of the New Testament ministries. He is the Source of all of the gifts that are given to the church. When all of the gifts are manifested and are free to flow in a church, then that church is open to the entire ministry of Jesus. If all of the gifts are not functioning, then we are not yet open to all of Him. The testimony of Christ is confirmed when no gifts are lacking and this testifies that we have made room for the complete work of Christ in our midst.

Gifts are not toys; they are tools for accomplishing the work of the Spirit. Those who function in the gifts and ministries of the Spirit have simply become vessels through whom the Lord may reach to touch the needs of His people. Jesus was THE Apostle, THE Prophet, THE Evangelist, THE Pastor and THE Teacher. He functioned in all of the gifts of the Spirit. When He ascended and gave gifts to men, He was in fact giving Himself to men. We cannot recognize a teacher by how well he can expound the Scriptures or articulate sound doctrine but we must see our Teacher in them. We cannot recognize a true pastor by his degrees, or even by who may have commissioned him, but only by seeing our Shepherd in him. The release of gifts and ministries in our churches is simply the release of the Lord Himself into our midst.

We must wake up to our true condition and repent of our disobedience, or we will be removed and our callings given to those who will bear the fruit. For all of the preaching and teaching on equipping the saints, it is not getting done. Knowing the truth has not resulted in our walking in truth. This does not bring a blessing; it brings judgment.

As the apostle stated, all of the equipping ministries are given for the equipping of the saints to do the work of the ministry. Even the evangelist, who we tend to think of as sent to the lost, has the primary function of equipping the saints for evangelism because the whole church is called to that work. If the evangelist is not producing other evangelists and a spirit of evangelism in the church, he is not accomplishing his primary function. The same is true of the prophet. His primary function is to equip the saints to speak for God. This does not mean that all will function in the office of prophet; but anyone may be used of God to prophesy and to have visions, dreams, etc. Even the pastor is not just called to guide the people but to reproduce in the church the Spirit of the Shepherd that we would all become our brother's keepers. No ministry is truly bearing fruit unless it is REPRODUCING "after its own kind."

There is more than enough ministry to go around. We must not be threatened by others who start to walk in our ministries, even if they are more effective than we are. The most perfect type of true spiritual ministry is found with John the Baptist. His whole purpose was to prepare the way for Jesus, to testify of Him, and then to be willing to decrease as He increased. This is why a man who performed no miracles, expounded no new truths, and left no institution was called by the Son Of God "the greatest man ever born of woman." This is the nature of those who are true friends of the Bridegroom.

The whole church is called to be an apostle (one sent by God), a prophet (one who speaks for God) an evangelist (bearer of the good news), a shepherd (our brother's keeper), and a teacher (able to instruct others in the ways of God).

## Forsake Not the "Assembling"

The Biblical admonition to "forsake not the assembling" was not just referring to meetings, but the joining together of the different parts of the body. The Lord sees only one church. The Lord's people are going to be freed from the spirit of division which emphasizes differences instead of our common purpose. A severe judgment is coming upon all who separate instead of join, who are in fact building for themselves instead of for Him. This includes individuals, local churches, as well as denominations and the different streams flowing within the church. Satan came to divide and destroy. The fundamental purpose of the Kingdom of God is synthesis: the joining together to form one whole. But we must understand that this synthesis will never be accomplished through human agency; it can come only by the Spirit.

Presently there are a number of different "streams" in the body of Christ, each with its own different leadership and emphasis. Presently the different streams are in the Lord's purpose, but ultimately all of them will flow together into one River. At that time this River will swell to become an irresistible force before which no other religion, philosophy, or doctrine can stand.

The body of Christ is presently like the designing of a giant airplane. There are groups of engineers working on each system: one group designing the landing gear, another the engines, another the wings, etc. Most of the engineers can only see and understand their part, which is all they need to understand at this time. Only a few know the plans for the entire plane; these are committed to the task of being sure that all of the different systems and parts will interface properly when it is time to fit them together. The work of those few who are committed to the interfacing will not be evident until the day the plane is completed and rolled out for display. Then everyone will see their section as essential to the whole but also as just one little part.

In this same way, those in the different streams have been accomplishing their purpose. Most did not need to see the whole plan, but the day has now come for the interfacing to begin. This must happen if any are to be used by the Lord in the future. What good would any part of the plane be without the rest of it? The Lord is now beginning to send forth those who see the entire plan. These are working to establish interrelations between the different streams so that when the time comes, the "wing" will fit properly with the "fuselage," etc.

It is time for interchange to begin, but we must be careful not to force a mating of the sections before they're ready. The Lord has not allowed the different sections of this plane to come together yet because there are still men in leadership who would try to fly it, and He will be its only pilot. As this interchange begins, we must understand that every part will not be directly joined to every other part. The arm must be joined to the shoulder, not the hip. Ultimately all of the parts will be joined, but many will be joined *through* other parts, possibly not having much of a direct relationship. It can be a futile waste of time for us to try to join with every other stream in the church. We must be sensitive to give ourselves only to the relationships the Lord is establishing for us.

The dismantling of organizations and disbanding of some works will be a positive and exhilarating experience for the faithful servants. They will not just be leaving something behind, they will be going on to a much greater work. Those who have fallen to worship the work of God more than the God of the work will have trouble, but most of these too will be set free by the tremendous anointing which is coming.

## Beware of Stumbling Blocks

Many who feel called to attack and tear down the old institutions or denominations will not be sent from God. There will be "stumbling blocks" circulating in the church who will cause confusion and some destruction from time to time. They will perceive themselves as prophets sent to judge and deliver, but they will in fact be sent by the evil one to divide and destroy. Those serving in leadership must trust their discernment and must remove the stumbling blocks.

To be distinguished from the stumbling blocks, the Lord will raise up a great company of apostles, prophets, evangelists, pastors and teachers who will have the spirit of Phinehas. Just as the son of Eleazar could not tolerate iniquity in the camp of the Lord, this "ministry of Phinehas" will save congregations, and at times cities and nations, from the plagues that will be sweeping the earth (See Numbers 25:1-13). They will be moved by the jealousy of the Lord for the purity of His people. They will be sent to save and preserve the work of the Lord, not to tear down like the stumbling blocks.

As part of the Lord's preparation for bringing the church together, there will be an increasing emphasis on walking in sanctification. This is to be distinguished from the legalistic devotion to externals, the decrees the apostle warned about such as, **"Do not handle, do not taste, do not touch"** (Colossians 2:21). We are exhorted to, **"Pursue peace with all men, and the sanctification *without which no one will see the Lord"*** (Hebrews 12:14). Sin separates; it separates us from God and from each other. The Lord will no longer tolerate the lusts of the flesh, the conniving of the soul, or the pollution of spirit which has dominated His people. His judgment upon these things is coming with severity just as the prophet Malachi warned:

> **"For behold, the day is coming, burning like a furnace, and all the arrogant and every evildoer will be like chaff; and the day that is coming will set them ablaze," says the Lord of Hosts, "so that it will leave them neither root nor branch. But for you WHO FEAR MY NAME the Sun of Right-eousness will rise with healing in His wings [lit."rays"]; and you will go forth and skip about like calves from the stall. And you will tread down the wicked, for they shall be as ashes under the soles of your feet on the day which I am prepar-ing," says the Lord of Hosts"** (Malachi. 4:1-3).

## False Unity Movements

There will be unity movements started which are not ordained by the Holy Spirit. Some of these will bring in-creased division and confusion to the church. Some of these will have been originated by deceivers seeking control and coming in the spirit of anti-Christ. Some will be started by true believers who have foreseen what is to come but will be deluded into thinking they are the chosen vessels to bring it about. There will be so much confusion born out of these false movements that for a time the body of Christ will get sick of the very word "unity."

There will be many relatively small false unity movements resulting in discord, but there will be one great and significant movement which will ultimately become the greatest persecutor of the advancing church. This movement will be a marriage of Catholics, Protestants, Evangelicals, Pentecostals, Charismatics and Third Wave Christians. This movement will gain momentum after a period of great humiliation for the church (this is elaborated on in later chapters). It will have all of the appearance of being God's vehicle for reestablishing the respectability and credibility of the church when in fact it will be the primary vehicle for anti-Christ forces trying to thwart the harvest.

True unity will not come through any person or movement seeking to bring about unity. It will *not* come through ecumenical movements, political compromises, or the attempt by men to bring about unity, regardless of how noble these may seem. As Martin Luther once observed: "Spiritual men do not need a covenant; unspiritual men cannot keep one." Unity will not even come about through persecution. As history testifies, persecution will cause Christians to lay aside differences for a season, but as soon as the persecution is lifted, they again quickly separate because this kind of unity is often more the result of external conditions than a true change in heart. The unity the Spirit is bringing about will weather all conditions and environments because it will not be dependent on environment, but on the Spirit.

What is coming will go beyond human contracts and political agreements. As the Lord prayed in John 17:22: **"The GLORY which thou hast given Me I have given to them;**

**that they may be one, just as We are one."** True unity can only come when the church sees the Glory of the Lord Himself. As Isaiah foresaw: **"Darkness will cover the earth, and deep darkness the peoples, but THE LORD WILL RISE UPON YOU, AND HIS GLORY WILL APPEAR UPON YOU"** (Isaiah 60:2). When the church beholds the glory of the Lord, which she will do, like the twenty-four elders in Revelation 4:10-11, all crowns will be cast at His feet. Who could presume glory or position in His presence? When we see the Lamb as He is, our pettiness and pretensions will be causing all of us to grovel for mercy and to repent for the things we have done to injure or divide His people.

Those who enter into the unity of the true Spirit will not even be aware of it; their attention will not be on the church and what she is attaining but on the Lord Himself. The advancing church is soon to rise above worshipping the temple of the Lord to worshipping the Lord of the temple. This is what will result in true unity.

There has been a fundamental deception promulgated throughout the body of Christ which has tried to focus our attention on who we are in Christ instead of Who He is in us. We do need to know who we are in Him, but when that becomes our emphasis, we will never become who He has called us to be. We are not changed by seeing ourselves. It is by beholding His glory that we are changed into His image, which is the image the church is called to bear.

There will be a great movement to return the church the Biblical simplicity for church life, structure and government. But let us understand that neither the Lord nor the apostolic authors of Scripture left us with a clear formula for church structure—purposely! To have done so would have robbed the church of the very life force that indeed makes her the church—Christianity is not a formula, it is a relationship with Christ. The church is not the pattern for the church; Jesus is the pattern for the church. The unity of the church will never come from everyone finally deciding to do everything the same way—it will only come when we all start following the same One.

*Chapter 5*

# The Judgment Begins

**For it is time for judgment to begin with the household of God. (I Peter 4:17)**

**But when we are judged, we are disciplined by the Lord in order that we may not be condemned along with the world. (I Corinthians 11:32)**

One of the Greek words translated "judgment" is "krisis," from which we derive our English word "crisis." This is not for punishment or condemnation; it is to purify the church so that she will be found standing on a sure foundation when judgment comes upon the world, **"in order that we may not be condemned along with the world."** It is so that we may be light for the world when she enters the greatest time of darkness. We cannot pull anyone else out of the quicksand unless we are on solid ground ourselves.

One of the definitions for *crisis* is "the point in a disease at which it is determined if a patient will live or die." This is a good explanation of the judgment the church, and then the world, is about to go through. Everything which can be shaken will be; everything that is not gold, silver, or precious stones will be burned. **"Each man's work will become evident; for the DAY will show it, because it is to be**

**revealed with fire; and the fire itself will test the quality of each man's work"** (I Corinthians 3:13).

The judgment that is coming will separate the wheat from the tares in the church, and in the individuals who remain in the church. There is not a Christian in the world who will not be humbled to some degree by this fire. There is also not a Christian in the world who will not benefit to become more pure in life and intimate with the Lord. It will not be easy but it will be worth it.

## Grace and False Grace

There will not be one who can stand in what is coming except by God's grace. But His grace will be sufficient for all who call upon Him. He will give us His power and His wisdom. This fire will also judge those who presume upon false grace, which is the presumption that His grace is the continual overlooking of irresponsibility and sin. He is coming to judge sin and condemn it in all of its forms. Those who have heard His words, but have not acted on them, will be washed away with the storm. Let us not be like the foolish virgins who did not keep oil in their lamps, presuming that they could get some when the bridegroom came. Those who are so foolish will find themselves locked out. Presumption is the foundation of a false doctrine of grace, and that foundation will quickly be found inadequate.

God's judgment, which comes in the form of crisis, works in the church continually, and in every believer's life continually, to some degree. Every problem we have in life is meant to move us toward the true grace and power of God. But the crisis that is coming before the end is to a much greater degree than anything experienced before. As the Lord Jesus warned: **"For then there will be a great tribulation, such as has not occurred since the beginning of the world until now, nor ever shall"** (Matthew 24:21). But along with this great tribulation there will also be great grace and power available to the church—a greater grace and a greater power than she has ever known before. This we also see in Isaiah 60:1-2:

> **Arise, shine; for your light has come, and the glory of the Lord has risen upon you. For behold, darkness will cover the earth, and deep darkness the peoples; but the Lord will rise upon you, and His glory shall appear upon you.**

At the very time when darkness is covering the earth, and deep darkness the peoples, the Lord is rising upon His people, and His glory is appearing upon them. This is the ultimate clash between the light and the darkness, and the light will prevail. This will be the greatest hour for the church that all of the righteous men and women in history have longed to see. The judgment, or crisis, that is coming upon the church first, is to prepare her for the greatest glory she will ever know. The fire of this tribulation will prepare her for the glory—the glory will transform the church into a pure and spotless bride that is worthy of the Lord.

*There is an easier way through this tribulation.* Before the Lord sends His judgment in the form of crisis, He will send a clear warning to His people so that we can judge ourselves so that he will not have to judge us. It is better to fall on the Rock and be broken than to have the Rock fall on us and be ground into powder. If we would devote ourselves to the discipline of a holy and pure life, repent and remove the sin that has entangled us in so many ways, we will not have to endure the crisis that is prepared. As Peter stated it in I Peter 1:6-7: **"In this you greatly rejoice, even though now for a little while, *if necessary,* you have been distressed by various trials, that the proof of your faith, being more precious than gold which is perishable, even though tested by fire, may be found to result in praise and glory and honor at the revelation of Jesus Christ."**

Note the words "if necessary" in verse 6. The reciprocal of this is that it is *not necessary* for all. If we would judge ourselves, discipline ourselves for godliness, we could escape many of even the everyday trials that we must now endure. If we will voluntarily fall on the Rock and be broken, He would not have to fall on us.

The Lord disciplines those whom He loves, and this judgment is coming because He loves us. We will all need the help of some crisis to get to the place where we can stand the flood that is coming. Even so, the Lord will give us warnings before He sends His trials so that we can make it as easy on ourselves as we can. The storm will come upon every house, but those who are hearing His words *and acting on them* will have built on the Rock and their houses will stand. Those who live in such houses need not fear the storms. If we have excessive fear about these things, we must not let it drive us to despair but to *do something* about our spiritual condition. As the psalmist warned: **"Therefore, let everyone who is godly pray to Thee in a time when Thou mayest be found; surely in a flood of great waters they shall not reach Him"** (Psalm 32:6).

We have been promised that if we seek the Lord we will find Him, but it will be too late to save our "houses" if we wait until the flood is upon us. We are choosing today both the judgment and the glory which will come to us.

## Paradise Now

As a prophetic message, metaphorically Jesus was crucified between two thieves who represented "yesterday" and "tomorrow." One of the robbers was in bondage to his past and to all of the evil he had done; the other had his attention on the future, saying: **"Lord, *when* you come into your kingdom..."** The Lord corrected his emphasis when He said **"*Today*, you will be with Me in Paradise"** (Luke 23:43).

It is apparent from the Scriptures that the Lord did not go that day to Paradise, but into the depths. Then what did He mean when He told the thief that "today" he would be with Him in Paradise? He is saying the same thing to us! Do not wait for tomorrow, *today* is the day of salvation. There is a revelation in knowing Him TODAY that touches eternity. Yesterday no longer exists; tomorrow does not exist either! The only thing that exists is the *present*.

Paradise must be found in the present; it is not some futuristic dream but a present reality. We must learn from our past and have a vision for the future, but we are not to live in them. That's why the exhortations are **"TODAY, if you hear His voice, do not harden your hearts"** (Hebrews 4:7), and **"At the acceptable time I listened to you, and on the day of salvation I helped you, behold NOW is the acceptable time, behold NOW is the day of salvation"** (II Corinthians 6:2). More important than knowing the future is abiding in Him TODAY. This is why, when Moses asked what name He would be known by, He said "I AM," not I WAS, or I WILL BE.

If we are to know Him, we must know Him in the present. The same two metaphorical thieves may well have stolen more of the life and power from the church than anything else. We must not let them steal any more. It does not matter how long we have known the Lord, how many times we have read the Bible, how many others we have led to Christ, if we are not abiding in Him TODAY. Neither does it matter how we failed yesterday, how far we backslid, even how we may have denied Him; if we repent, TODAY can be the day of our salvation, TODAY we can establish our lives upon the Rock. Our eternity will be decided TODAY! TODAY we too can be with Him in Paradise; we can be seated with Him in the heavenly places. Even though this vision was given to help prepare the church for future events, this knowledge will not do us any good if it does not change our lives TODAY.

## Deliverance From Judgment

Those who know the word of the Lord will not be saved by that knowledge; we must be doers of the Word. Many have come to know the way. A few more go on to know truth, but not many come to know Jesus as their LIFE, and that is what He came to give us. The Way is not a path or a formula, but a Person. The Truth is not an acknowledgment of certain Biblical and spiritual facts—Truth is a Person. We do not know the true Way or the Truth if we do not also know Him as our Life. Christianity is not an assimilation of or agreement with certain principles and facts—it is a relationship. That relationship alone can prepare us for what is to come, regardless of how accurately we may foresee the future. *The ONLY escape from the judgment is to be found in Christ.* The most accurate knowledge of truth or coming events will not help us if we are not abiding in Him.

One of the great failures of historic Christianity has been the tendency to substitute rituals for reality, form for substance, concepts and formulas for Life. We must each determine to cultivate a relationship with the Lord that is real and profound, a relationship that is the consuming and undivided concentration of our hearts.

A storm is soon coming upon the entire world, after which only those houses which were built upon the rock will remain "… **He has promised, saying, 'Yet once more will I shake not only the earth, but also the heaven;' and this expression, 'yet once more,' denotes the removing of those things which can be shaken, as of created things, in order that those things which cannot be shaken may remain,"** (Hebrews 12:26-27). This judgment is to remove that which is not of Him, but it is also for the purpose of establishing and purifying that which is of Him, so that it can remain.

The Lord is not coming back to condemn the world; it is already condemned! He is coming to build and establish His kingdom and authority and He will not build it upon the world's foundations. The land must first be cleared of everything which He has not built. "**Every plant which my heavenly father did not plant shall be rooted up**" (Matthew 15:13).

This judgment begins with the household of God for two basic reasons: 1) so that when the world falls apart we will be established in the strength of Christ and able to minister life and healing, and 2) because in many ways we need it more than the world does. The church has been prone to point the finger at the world for its sins, while living itself in the same idolatry of self-centeredness, though it did so from behind a cleaner facade.

An idol is not just something we worship, it is that which we trust in and give our attention to. During this time of relative peace and safety many have been lulled into a false security; a security which is not founded in Christ but in the world and its systems. The Lord is not impressed with religious exercises; one can teach a parrot to do and say the right things. He purchased us with His blood that "we who live should no longer live for ourselves but for Him." Anything less than this is idolatry.

When the rich young ruler wanted to follow Jesus he was required to give up all that he owned. A compromise would not have saved the young man, and nothing less will save us. As the Lord Himself declared, **"So therefore, no one of you can be My disciple who does not give up ALL of his own possessions"** (Luke 14:33). In order to make it easy for people to "make a decision for Christ," we have reduced the gospel to the point that it requires little or nothing from us, and by this we have destroyed its very power to save. These are false gospels which feed the self-centeredness and self-promotion which caused death to enter the world in the beginning and have been its perpetuating delusion, regardless of whether they are called the gospel or any other philosophy.

The day of reckoning will soon be upon us. Those for whom the decision was made so easy will soon find the Way intolerably difficult. These will not only fall away in the days to come, they will become some of the most unrelenting enemies of the true church. We have done no one a favor by reducing the cost of discipleship. Those who thought they could come and still save their self-lives will lose them anyway. Only those who have truly lost their lives to find Him will stand the day that is coming.

## Spiritual Immorality and Spiritual Abortion

The church has been pointing its finger at the world for its immorality even while she commits spiritual immorality with the world. As James declared: **"You adulteresses, do you not know that friendship with the world is hostility toward God? Therefore whoever wishes to be a friend of the world makes himself an ENEMY OF GOD"** (James 4:4). How many of us would have married our spouses if on our wedding day they had vowed to be utterly faithful to us 364 days a year, and to be unfaithful only one day a year? Is it any different in our relationship to the Lord?

We abhor abortions (as we should), but how many spiritual seeds planted in the church by the Lord have been aborted because we didn't want to bother with carrying them to term? How many potentially great and effective men and women of God are now lifeless pew warmers because we snuffed out the vision God had planted in them for ministry? How many of our neighbors would have been born again into the kingdom if we had not aborted God's leading to go talk to them?

We have been quick to point our finger at the world for its abortions while we commit spiritual abortion for the same reasons as theirs: we are selfish, it is too inconvenient to carry the spiritual seeds to term, or we do not think we can afford them. How many of God's seeds for missions have we aborted before they were even born because we could not afford to send them out, while at the same time we gloat over our new multi-million dollar buildings and family life centers.

The Lord does hate abortion, and it will bring His wrath, but He is going to start with His own house. If the church were walking in the light that she has, the world would not be living in such darkness. We flail at the world's branches, but the Lord is about to put the ax to the root of our own tree. The church is called to confront the world about its iniquity, but not before we have been examined by the same finger. Only then will we be able to effectively confront the world and its problems. As the apostle explained, **"And we are ready to punish all disobedience,** *whenever your obedience is complete***"** (II Corinthians 10:6).

## Spiritual Homosexuality

Like immorality and abortion, homosexuality is a symptom of a much greater spiritual disease. The Scriptures establish that homosexuality is a perversion and is called an abomination to the Lord. There are but a few sins that are declared an abomination, which reflects their particular offensiveness to the Lord. He does not view "abominations" as "just another sin." Homosexuality is not just another form of lust. The Lord destroyed Sodom because of this perversion and some of the most serious judgment the world is going to suffer is because of this same sin. Even so, the Lord does love homosexuals and wants to save them, not condemn them. But salvation begins with recognition of the sin and the Lord is going to draw a sharp sword against this particular sin.

As Paul explained in Romans Chapter One, homosexuality if the result of having fallen from worshipping the Creator to worshipping the creature. Because the church is called to be the "salt of the earth," and the "light of the world," often the prevailing sins in the world are a reflection of the church's own spiritual sin or failures, which is the case with homosexuality. This perversion is the result of departing from true worship and much of the church has departed from true worship, at least to some degree. The degree of this departure can be measured by the degree to which homosexuality is spreading and capturing men and women.

So how has the church departed from true worship? Basically by starting to worship the church of the Lord in place of the Lord of the church. The church is a "creature," it is created. It is created with a glorious purpose to be the habitation of the Lord, but we have fallen to giving more attention to the Lord's house than to Him. This is a root of the sectarian spirit that has divided the church and perverted worship. We worship that which has our heart, and though we should all have a heart for the church, this must never exceed the devotion that we give to the Lord Himself or we have fallen from true worship to idolatry.

Homosexuality is having relations with your own sex. "Spiritual homosexuality" is also the desire to have relations only with our own kind. The Lord spelled this "homo-sect-uality." This is not meant to just be a funny play on words—it is a deadly serious condition in the church. Sectarianism is self-centeredness, self-seeking and self-preservation that is the result of self-worship.

A.I.D.S. is part of the judgment that is coming upon the world for its homosexuality and its perversions. A.I.D.S is the breakdown of the body's natural defenses against disease. No one really dies from A.I.D.S, they die from the diseases that the body can no longer defend against because of the A.I.D.S. Simple illnesses that the body usually fights off easily, can become fatal when the natural defenses have been destroyed. Churches that are spiritually homosexual, or sectarian, are likewise becoming subject to a spiritual form of A.I.D.S. Congregations, movements, or denominations, that are sectarian are going to become increasingly subject to a "spiritual virus" that will likewise break down their defense systems. Problems that before would have been easily handled will then become deadly. Just as the literal A.I.D.S. is destined to become increasingly deadly, with new forms being released and taking the lives of millions, if the church does not repent of her spiritual homosexuality many now vibrant congregations, movements and even whole denominations will be lost.

If homosexuality goes unchecked, it will become one of the greatest threats to religious freedom in the world. The church will be nearly defenseless against this spirit until she repents of her own sectarianism, which is her own spiritual homosexuality, and returns to worshipping the Creator instead of His creations. Homosexuality is the sin that most reflects man's fall from true worship. The removal of homosexuality will come when we have returned to true worship, which will itself remove our sectarianism.

Many of the world's great artists are homosexuals. This lifestyle is so prevalent in the artist community because, to a large degree, art as a form of true worship has been rejected by much of the church. Art, in its pure form, is a reflection of the Lord's nature as the Master Creator. The universe is the Lord's canvas and He delights in the diversity and beauty of His creation. He delights in making every snowflake different, every person different, every day different. Yet the church is generally one of the most confined, predictable, boring and void of spontaneity of any institution on earth. This is because of our departure from true worship.

Art, by its creative nature, must always seek the new, the fresh, and push back the outer limits. Therefore, the artist is often in danger of crossing the line into error or perversion. But without the freedom of the artist, we are already captured by the dead form that has no life. When the church has returned to true worship, true art will have also been recovered and promoted by the church as one form of that worship. This is an art that transcends glorifying the creation to that which imparts awe and wonder of the blessed Creator that is reflected through the wonders of His creation.

The Lord Jesus said that the publicans and harlots would enter the kingdom of God before the Pharisees and other most righteous men in Israel. The demonic religious spirit that worked in the prevailing religion of that day was farther from the heart of God than many of the great sinners of the land. In the same way, homosexuals and radical artists who have fallen to some of the lowest forms of perversion are still in fact much closer to the true worship of God than many churches.

It is because of this that Satan will increasingly try to put both the art and the homosexual communities at enmity with the church in order to make the chasm between them much greater. But the Lord is going to raise up Christian leaders with the vision to recapture true art for the church, which is the rightful property of the church. These will have to brave brutal assaults from religious paranoids, but the domain that is retaken will be worth the price.

The second step that must be taken by the church to turn back the tide of homosexuality, is to love the sinners. True spiritual authority is founded upon love. Satan will not cast out Satan. We will not cast out homosexuality with fear, resentment, bitterness, or rejection. The church must love homosexuals because the Lord does, even though He despises and will judge the sin. When we can truly love them and at the same time stand uncompromisingly against the sin of homosexuality, the church will have authority to deliver the homosexual from this bondage and cast it out of the world.

In this way both art and homosexuality are, in a sense, barometers in society that measure how bright and pure is the light of the church that is shining. The true worship of God will turn men from homosexuality. The true worship of God is fueled by a creativity that will make all perverted art forms pale and uninteresting by comparison.

## Chapter 6

# Jonah, Laodicea and the Last Day Ministry

In many ways, the church in the West has been like Jonah fleeing from the presence of the Lord in the ship going to Tarshish. Tarshish represents the fields of ministry that God has not chosen. In many ways, religious activity has been substituted for obedience and the presence of the Lord. Many of the good works being accomplished by the church today truly are good works—they just are not the works that we have been called to. These good works are offered to God as a compensation for not doing what Hc has called us to do.

It was Jonah's rebellion that brought the storm upon the heathen in the ship; the church's rebellion and tendency to go the wrong way is the reason for many of the storms that are bringing much of the judgment upon the world today. The heathen in Jonah's story were actually more in touch with reality than was the man of God—they were trying to find God while the prophet slept! The heathen had to wake up the prophet so he could call on his God. Likewise, many of the heathen in the world have been more discerning of the times, false teaching and corruption in ministries than the church has been, and much of their slander and abuse that is hurled at the church is an attempt to wake her up so that she will call on her God.

This is not to imply that the world will not also be judged for its evil. It will be judged but not until the church has been. As the popular saying goes, "Having a ship in the sea is fine, but when the sea gets in the ship, we have a problem!" The church is presently being impacted more by the world than she is impacting the world. We must remove the ungodly influences from the church before she will have authority against ungodliness. As the apostle asked the Corinthians, **"Do we not judge those who are in the church?"** God's love is not the "sloppy agape" we have pretended it to be. When we give approval to the things which God disapproves of, it is unsanctified mercy, and it will bring judgment upon the whole house.

When Jesus walked on the earth Israel was certainly the most moral and upstanding nation in the world. As we see in the gospels they stoned those who were caught in adultery; they did not tolerate such sin in their midst. Yet the Lord said that it would be more tolerable for Tyre, Sidon and even Sodom in the day of judgment than for such apparently righteous cities as Chorazin, Bethsaida, and Capernaum (see Matthew 11:20-24). Tyre and Sidon were two of the most wicked cities of that time, and Sodom was one of the most wicked cities of all time, yet the moral and conservative cities of Israel are going to be worse off in the judgment than they were! Why? Because obviously God is not going to judge just by how much darkness there is, but by how much light has been rejected.

Chorazin, Bethsaida and Capernaum may have been moral and conservative, but they rejected the Light Himself when He came to offer them light. How much light has been offered to the church, and how much have we rejected? With greater light comes greater accountability. We tend to measure ourselves by the rest of the world and thereby think that we rate highly, but God does not measure us by the world—He looks at how much light He has given to us and how much we are walking in. Considering the standards He gave to the cities of Israel, how is He going to measure us?

A fire is soon coming upon the church which will remove the wood, hay and stubble, but it will leave behind gold, silver and precious stones. Of the works that were done in the Lord's name but not by His commission, not one stone will be left upon another. *Everything that can be shaken, will be shaken.* That which is His will be purified, that which is not His will be removed. There is not a church, a ministry, a minister, or an individual who will not be touched by this fire. We will all be humbled before the Lord, before each other, and before the world. Pride and presumption started the fall, and its removal from the church will end her fall and begin her exaltation. This is necessary because the greatest exaltation of the church in history is to follow this judgment.

We can make our judgment easier. By the Lord's mercy He is going to send a clear word of warning to His people that we might judge ourselves before He has to judge us. "Mercy triumphs over judgment" and the Lord would rather show mercy. He would rather that our discipline be as easy on us as possible, but He is going to have a holy people. If mercy does not work, if we do not come to repentance because of His kindness, His wrath will follow.

Neither let us not presume that ignorance will excuse us. Everyone will have an opportunity to hear His warning, but those who are so caught up in their own affairs or distractions that they do not take time to listen will pay a terrible price for their neglect. Their judgment will be just—there will be no excuse for anyone. Now is the time for us to repent of our lukewarmness and self-seeking. Let us not keep pointing at the darkness the world is living in if our own light is not shining for them. Let us now return to our first love and our first commitment and never let them be stolen from us again.

## Laodicea

The seven churches in Revelation were a prophetic parallel of the entire church age. Seven is often used as the number of completion in Scripture and the seven churches reflect the complete, historic church. Beginning with Ephesus, which portrayed the first century church, we can see a remarkable outline of church history. Laodicea, being the last of the seven churches, is a type of the last day church. We usually think of Laodicea as the lukewarm church and that is indeed our primary problem. We think that we are wealthy, and we are more wealthy than any church in history in many ways, but in true life and power we are poor and blind and naked. Even though the Laodicean church received such a devastating verdict of its condition, *the greatest promises given to any of the churches were given to the Laodicean church if she would overcome.* We esteem highly those who overcome during times of persecution, darkness and evil, as we should, but the greatest overcomers of all may be those who have overcome the lukewarmness generated by prosperity and comfort.

In Revelation 3:20 we see the Lord knocking at the door of the Laodicean church seeking to personally come in and dine with her. It is noteworthy that the Lord is outside trying to get in! Even so, He is seeking to enter and to personally give this church more revelation and truth than to any other church in history. Not only do we have the Bible compiled, but it is now freely available in almost every major country in the world. We have nearly universal literacy, books, tapes, videos, radio, television and have been blessed with some of the most extraordinary teachers in church history.

A man of God can spend his entire life acquiring knowledge and explain it in a book which we can absorb in a few hours. Yet are we using this great knowledge, or do we even appreciate the incredible blessing that the Lord has made available to us today? Every seeker of God in history would love to have had what He has given to us, and we have been most lukewarm in our appreciation and use of it. The time has come to arise from our stupor, open the door, and let the Lord into His own church.

What does it means to dine "with Jesus"? After His resurrection even His most intimate disciples had trouble recognizing Him. It is because they were more dependent upon their knowledge of His physical appearance than His heart—they knew Him after the flesh and not after the Spirit. After joining two of His disciples on the road to Emmaus, they did not recognize Him even when He opened the Scriptures to them. It was not until they saw Him *breaking the bread* that their eyes were opened. The same is true with us. It is when we see Jesus breaking our bread to feed us—not just our pastor, our favorite author, teacher, or televangelist, but the Lord Himself, that our eyes are opened. Of course the Lord uses these servants to speak to us, but we must start to recognize Him as the One who is feeding us.

It is not just hearing the words of the Lord that matters, but hearing the Word Himself. This is the promise to Laodicea, the last day church: if we hear *Him* knocking and open, we will dine *with Him*. Has this not been the desire of our hearts from the beginning: not just to know about Him, but to know Him, to commune with Him? He is our first love and we will return to Him. This is how the light, the glory and the power to accomplish the last day ministry will come—when our eye again becomes single upon Him, then the whole body will be full of light.

## Benjamin and the Last Day Church

There is a prophetic unfolding that parallels church history in the sons of Jacob, who were to become the twelve tribes of Israel. We can see a parallel of church history in the prophecies spoken over these twelve by both Jacob and

Moses. The church is the spiritual seed of Israel, and the history of the nation of Israel was a prophetic outline of the church's destiny—we see the natural revealed first and then the spiritual. We can see in Reuben, the first-born of Jacob, a portrayal of the early church. The birth of the following sons and the histories of the tribes derived from them comprises a remarkable picture of church history right down to Benjamin, the last son born and a type of the last day church.

Benjamin is one of three men in Scripture who was born in Bethlehem, the other two being David and Jesus. Bethlehem means "house of bread," or "a place of food," which again reflects the fact that the last day church would be born in the place of abundant spiritual food. When Benjamin and his brothers were invited to eat with Joseph in Egypt, before he had revealed his identity to them, the Scripture says, **"And he (Joseph) took portions to them from his own table; but Benjamin's portion was five times as much as any of theirs..."** (Genesis 43:34). This was another prophetic incident foretelling the abundant spiritual food to be provided for the last day church.

This abundance of spiritual food in this day exceeds all that of the other church ages and we must take advantage of this great opportunity. The knowledge, understanding, and outpouring of direct revelation from the Lord is given to us for a reason. We are going to need every bit of it to accomplish the mandate given to us in this hour. It is time to buy from Him the gold that has been refined by fire, those treasures of wisdom and knowledge that have been proven. It is time to buy from Him the garments of purity that will cover our sin and nakedness. It is time to buy from Him the eyesalve to open our eyes so that we can see from His perspective.

In Revelation 7:9, we see the great company clothed in white robes who stand before the throne. To the overcomers of the Laodicean church He promises that they will sit with

Him *on* His throne. He has made available to this church a position of authority and power that is unprecedented. This is not because of our righteousness but because of His purpose for these times. The authority He is about to give has never been needed before as it is now. Those who overcome the spirit of lukewarmness will soon do exploits unequaled in Old or New Testament times. The Lord has saved His best wine for last, and those who are zealous for Him are already beginning to partake of it. The glory of the latter house will be greater than that of the former (Haggai 2:9). This does not mean that the latter (last day) house is greater, but the glory in it will be greater.

We see this promise to the Laodicean overcomer also reflected in the life of Benjamin. When Benjamin was born, his mother died. Before she expired, she named him Benoni, which means "son of my sorrows." Jacob changed his name to Benjamin, which means "son of my right hand." He was transformed or "raised" from a son of sorrows to his mother to the son of his father's right hand. The right hand represents the position of authority and power as Jesus is seated at the right hand of the Father. That the last son was to be named Benjamin was a testimony of the authority with which the last day ministry would come forth.

Benjamin was the only one of the twelve who was named by his father and not his mother. This explains the authority that will be given to this last day ministry. They will not be named, or commissioned by their mother, the church, but by the Father. Their offices and ministries will not come because of the courses taken in seminary, nor will they be dictated by the pressing needs of the church or the people—they will receive their mandate from above. There are men and women alive today who have refused to receive their commissions from the church but are patiently waiting to hear the Father's voice saying, "This is My beloved Son as a teacher in you" (or apostle, prophet, etc.).

## The Cause of Burnout

The failure to wait for the Father's commission has resulted in much of the disorientation and spiritual burnout in ministries, which has in turn caused the lukewarm condition of the present church. This has caused potentially great evangelists to waste their lives trying to be pastors, or teachers trying to be evangelists, etc.

Others failed in ministry even though they knew their proper calling, but they mistook the *call* for the *commission*. There is a great difference between the calling of God to ministry and the commissioning to that ministry. Paul was called as an apostle many years before he was commissioned by the Holy Spirit. The time between the calling and the commissioning is crucial for the  proper preparation required for the ministry. As Paul explained, **"When He who had set me apart from my mother's womb, and *called* me through His grace, was pleased to reveal His Son IN me [not just TO him], that I might preach..."** (Galatians 1:15-16). Preparation is not just learning more about Him, or even His ways; it is having Jesus manifested *IN* us. Living waters come from the innermost being and only when Jesus is truly in our hearts, not just our minds, will we minister that which is in fact Jesus.

Miracles were performed by the Lord to confirm His word, but they were also meant to *be* a message. The first miracle He performed is one of the most important for us to understand. By His first miracle He was illustrating to the disciples just called what was the initial work to be done in them. He had the vessels set aside, which were typical of the disciples, and He had them filled to the brim with water. The water is typical of His word (see Ephesians 5:26) with which He was going to fill them. He then turned the water into wine symbolizing that He would turn His word into Spirit and Life in them. It is not enough to just have the correct mental understanding of His word; His word must become our life, that which fills our innermost being.

Anyone may teach about God's love, but only those who have laid down their lives with Him can impart that love. Anyone can teach truths but only those who have given their lives in search of it can impart a love for the truth, which is the essence of the true teaching ministry. The knowledge and ability to impart facts can easily be attained through study and practice; the apostolic ability to impart life can only be attained by taking up our crosses daily, following Him, like Him doing all things for the sake of the gospel, so that the message we bring is also our life.

For the last day ministry the Lord has set aside a number of "vessels" who have patiently waited for their water to be turned into wine. These are about to be released with such life and power in their message that the church will be just as stunned by its quality as the headwaiter was at the wedding in Cana. The Lord has again saved His best wine for last. After we have tasted it we will never again be content with the lifeless water of mere formulas and principles, contrived by the minds of those who substitute mental gymnastics for the ways of the Spirit.

Laodicea was exhorted to "be ZEALOUS therefore and repent," because a lack of zeal was a root of the problem. We must recognize the reasons for our lukewarmness if we are to be delivered from it. As stated, one significant cause is the present religious system which has put its own yokes on those trying to serve the Lord, forcing them into positions because of the needs of the church instead of their calling to a particular ministry. The Lord's yoke is the only yoke that we are called to carry. When we find the courage to resist the pressures of the people to do only that which the Lord has called us to do, we will have far more of that which is true life to give the people than we do now. Our tendency to carry the yokes of the people in place of the Lord's is certainly the major cause of burnout in ministry today.

## The Removal of Hype and Manipulation

Another reason for the lukewarmness of Laodicea is found in Jeremiah 50:6: **"My people have become lost sheep; their shepherds have led them astray. They have made them turn aside on the mountains; they have gone along from mountain to hill and have forgotten their resting place."**

Going from mountain to hill speaks of going from one thing that stimulates to the next, or from hype to hype; it is keeping the people excited but never leading them to the resting place, the Lord of the Sabbath Himself. This compulsion to keep people stimulated and moving is usually rooted in the insecurity in many who have prematurely entered the ministry, or who have departed from their particular realm of authority to try to do something they have not been commissioned to do. Instead of building on the solid rock of God's will, these usually substitute activity that is meant to keep a certain level of excitement in the people. These are usually driven by a fear that if the excitement level is not kept high the people will start scattering. But the church is weary of projects and hype and she now wants the Lord, as the preceding verses in Jeremiah explain:

> **In those days and at that time, declares the Lord, the sons of Israel will come, both they and the sons of Judah as well; they will go along weeping as they go, and IT WILL BE THE LORD THEIR GOD THEY WILL SEEK. They will ask for the way to Zion, turning their faces in its direction; THEY WILL COME THAT THEY MAY JOIN THEMSELVES TO THE LORD in an everlasting covenant that will not be forgotten (Jeremiah 50:4-5).**

The mega-ministries, projects and organizations that use hype and condemnation tactics to solicit support will not continue to receive the kind of response that they have in the past. Most of the church is becoming wise to the hype and manipulation that is so contrary to the Spirit of God. The church will not continue to be distracted by the "cities" which men build. She is now starting to look for the one built by God. The laborers about to be sent by the Lord will not just be builders of projects and ministries—they will build people, making "living stones" into a habitation for our God, that He might dwell among us.

The meaning of the name Laodicea reflects another reason for the lukewarmness now afflicting much of the church. Laodicea means "judging by the people." This could speak of at least two problems. First, of the critical, judgmental spirit which results in our separation from God and each other. Isaiah 58:9 says, **"Then you will call, and the Lord will answer; you will cry and He will say, 'Here I am,'** *if you remove the yoke from your midst, the pointing of the finger and speaking wickedness."*

When we are critical of the Lord's people we are in fact being critical of the Lord Himself. By this we are really saying that the Lord's workmanship in that person does not meet our standards. This is a grievous error that leads to a terrible darkness of soul. **"God resists the proud but gives His grace to the humble"** (James 4:6), and this kind of criticism is one of the most profound manifestations of pride—a pride that even judges God! Inevitably, the things of which we are the most critical in others are our own worst problems, or will be when the grace of God is removed from our lives because of this pride. By such judgment we keep ourselves in bondage.

Much of this is rooted in the power of the "two thieves" discussed earlier. We tend to keep others, and ourselves, in bondage to yesterday. The Lord is moving in and changing everyone who seeks Him. When we continue to relate to each other according to how we were, instead of giving each other the grace to be made new every day, we are making it more difficult for everyone to walk in the grace of God and in their renewed nature. This is a yoke that has resulted in much weariness, therefore lukewarmness, in this church age.

## The Wrong Form of Democracy

Another aspect of this "judging by the people" is the democratic spirit prevalent in the church. Because fallen men tend to be corrupted by power, democracy has proven to be the safest form of government for human affairs. Carried over into the church, it can be devastating and misleading. The kingdom of God is just that, a *kingdom*. Our king must be Lord of all or He will not be our Lord at all. Rule by committee or popular consensus has sent a great part of confessing Christendom down the deadly path to humanism.

A man once keenly observed, "Well if the Lord doesn't show up tonight we've got a pretty good program anyway!" Is that not what has happened? Unable to wait patiently for the Lord (which He always requires), we have determined to get something going to keep the people interested. Is this not what caused Aaron to make the golden calf? The people could not wait for Moses to come down from the mountain and they had to have something to get them going again. How many weak leaders, like Aaron, have given way to this pressure. How many golden calves, symbolic of carnal strength, now stand in our sanctuaries? An idol is not just a graven image, but it is anything that the people trust in place of the one true God. As with the golden calf, the time has come when the Lord is going to grind all of our substitutes for Him into powder.

# Part II

# *Kingdom Authority*

## Chapter 7

# The Nature
# of Spiritual Authority

When the people came to make Jesus king He fled to the mountains. We may consider this a noble intention on the part of the people, but it was in fact one of the most presumptuous acts recorded in Scripture. Mere men thought that they could make God king! If the people make you king who will rule? The people. Jesus could not be made king: He was BORN king.

The same is true of spiritual authority in ministry. If it is the people from whom we derive our authority they will be the ones who rule, not God. This is one of the primary reasons for the church's lack of power and authority. We have been taking men's yokes instead of the Lord's. A person only has true spiritual authority to the degree that the King reigns within him.

Before the church can walk in true prophetic authority she must take the position that Elijah did. When he first appeared to King Ahab his statement was, **"As the Lord, the God of Israel lives,** *before whom I stand...* **"** (I Kings 17:1). Elijah's statement that he was not standing before Ahab implied that he knew Ahab was just a man; it was the Lord who lives before Whom Elijah was standing—it was the Lord, not men, before Whom he lived his life. Until we learn that same lesson we cannot be entrusted with significant spiritual power and authority. It was Elijah's focus upon the "Living God" that enabled the Lord to trust him with such awesome power even to shut the heavens and call down fire from them.

## Overcoming the Fear of Man

To the degree that we are living our lives before the thrones of men we will be false in our ministry. As the apostle Paul explained **"For am I now seeking the favor of men, or of God? Or am I striving to please men?** *If I were still seeking to please men I would not be a bond servant of Christ"* **(Galatians 1:10).** Elijah knew better than to confuse God's approval with man's. The church has tended to confuse the need to be a witness to men and loving them with the compulsion to find its approval from men. This has been one of the most corrupting delusions sapping the church's ability to walk in true spiritual authority.

When defending his apostleship, the first point which Paul addressed was: **"Am I not free?"** (I Corinthians 9:1). Of what is an apostle required to be free? In another statement Paul claimed to be a slave of Christ. It is precisely by this slavery to Christ that we are freed to be sent by Him. As Isaiah stated: **"It is the Lord of hosts whom you should regard as holy. And He shall be your fear, and He shall be your dread,** *Then* **He shall become a sanctuary"** (Isaiah 8:13-14). If we have the true and holy fear of the Lord we will not fear anything else. Then He becomes our sanctuary! Then our work will be untainted by human motives and self-promotion.

The apostolic commission of Paul was destined to arouse the rage and opposition not only of the religious establishment but of the entire Roman Empire. This frail earthen vessel charged unrelentingly into the face of the most powerful principalities and powers of his age, with so little compromise or consideration for his own life that he shook those powers to their very foundations. The Roman officials exclamation that Paul was turning the world upside down was an accurate comprehension of the power of apostolic preaching. This preaching shakes the powers in heaven and earth, and it will solicit their most vehement wrath. Freedom from the fear of man and demon is a prerequisite for true ministry.

Jesus declared, **"You are those who justify yourselves in the sight of men, but God knows your hearts; for that which is highly esteemed among men is detestable in the sight of God"** (Luke 16:15). We have a choice to make; if we want to be esteemed by men we will be doing that which is detestable to God. The degree to which we seek to please and gain the acceptance of men is the degree to which our message will be diluted, and it will be detestable in our Lord's eyes, regardless of how piously we may use His name. As Jesus exhorted: **"Woe to you when all men speak well of you, for in the same way their fathers used to treat the false prophets!"** (Luke 6:26).

In order to preach an apostolic message it has to be settled in our hearts whose approval we are seeking: God or man's. As Jesus asked His disciples, **"How can you believe, when you receive glory from one another, and do not seek the glory that is from the one and only God?"** (John 5:44). Seeking glory from one another is possibly a most destructive force which erodes true faith. As the Lord questioned, "How can you believe" when you do this? The compulsion to have the acceptance of men erodes our faith as well as the message.

It was for this reason that Paul had to rebuke Peter, the first apostle to preach the resurrection of Jesus, **"because he stood condemned."** (Galatians 2:11-14). Peter had compromised the straightforwardness of the gospel because he feared the Jewish believers. This same tendency had previously compelled Jesus to call Peter "Satan," because he was setting his mind on man's interests instead of God's (see Matthew 16:21-23).

## Removing Unnecessary Stumbling Blocks

Spiritual authority demands freedom from the fear of man, but this freedom must be salted with the wisdom to avoid being unnecessarily offensive. This is what Paul meant when he said, **"For though I am free from all men, I have made myself a slave to all,** *that I might win more.* **To the Jews I became as a Jew, that I might win Jews..."** (I Corinthians 9:19-20). Paul adjusted his lifestyle somewhat to the customs of those he was trying to reach, not because he feared them or wanted their approval but because he loved them and wanted to save them. There are compromises that we may be called on to make in our lifestyle, but never with our morality, or our commitment to obey the Holy Spirit. These compromises are made for love's sake, not fear, or self-seeking.

## The Mount of Transfiguration

The second point which Paul used to establish his authority was **"Have I not** *seen* **the Lord?"** This is another primary prerequisite for true spiritual authority. We must challenge ourselves with this same question. Who are we seeing, Ahab or the living God?

The Mount of Transfiguration is a good example of why our vision must be concentrated on Jesus and not men. Jesus took Peter, James and John up to a high mountain (see Matthew 17:1-8). Jesus was transfigured and Moses and Elijah appeared talking to Him. This was a testimony that the ministries of Moses (the law) and Elijah (the prophets) spoke of Him and continued to speak to Him. Upon seeing this great revelation Matthew records, **"And Peter** *answered.*" Nobody was even talking to Peter! This often gets us into similar trouble. We think we know so much that we start talking and making plans before we even understand what the revelation means. Peter's reaction was a common human response to a great spiritual revelation: **"Lord, it is good for us to be here, *I WILL*..."** (v.4). Peter's good intention was in fact an echo of Satan himself personified in Isaiah 14: **"*I WILL* ascend to heaven. *I WILL* raise my throne. *I WILL*..."**

The good of the Tree of Knowledge is just as deadly as the evil because they both have the same root. As Paul explained to the men of Athens, **"Human hands cannot serve Him"** (Acts 17:25). History is littered with the refuse of great spiritual revelations that, instead of shaking and challenging the kingdoms of this world, went on to be absorbed by them, actually increasing the dominion of Babylon instead of the Kingdom of God.

It was good for Peter to be on that mountain, but not for the reasons that he presumed. It was good for him to hear the rebuke of the Father, **"This is My beloved Son, HEAR HIM!"** It was good for Peter to have the fear of God overshadow him after his great presumption. The result of this rebuke is the Lord's desire for us all: **"And lifting up their eyes, they saw no one, EXCEPT JESUS HIMSELF, ALONE"** (v.8). Jesus ALONE must be the vision of those who would be apostolic.

## Handling the Glory

The glory of the Lord will be revealed *to* His people, and then *upon* them. In some cases this will be an actual visible manifestation. His presence will be known until His nearness is the consuming desire of our hearts. As He draws near to us there will be almost no attention or concern given to the temples we have made, the works, projects, the campaigns and hype which have so wearied and burdened the church and have been a primary cause for the prevailing lukewarmness.

But this glory is not being revealed just to give us more work to do—it is coming to change us into the image of the Lord.

The glory is not being revealed so that we can build tabernacles for it. When it comes our whole job is going to be to behold it, let it change us, let it work in us a true worship that is in Spirit and truth. Then the glory will be revealed in us and accomplish far more for the purposes of the Lord than any projects we could give ourselves to. When the Lord again has just a few men who are truly Christlike, He will again shake the foundations of this world with His glory.

After the resurrection of Jesus, Peter and some of the disciples decided to go fishing. They labored all night and caught nothing. The next morning the Lord appeared on the bank and told them to cast their nets on the other side. Immediately their nets were full. Peter, realizing that it was the Lord, jumped into the sea and swam ashore. After spending just a few minutes in the presence of Jesus, Peter then went down and by himself drew in the net that all of the other disciples had been struggling with. A few minutes in His presence will empower us to accomplish far more than multiplied human effort.

The apostle Paul gave to the Corinthians a warning that remains universally appropriate for every church—**"But I am afraid, lest as the serpent deceived Eve by his craftiness, your minds should be led astray from the simplicity and purity of devotion to Christ"** (II Corinthians 11:3).

We can actually be distracted from the ultimate purpose of God by the lesser purposes of God. This happens when the lesser purposes eclipse the ultimate, or primary purpose. We are not called to *do* as much as we are called to *be*—Christlike. If the ministry spent as much time, energy and resources building people as it did building things, the light of the truth that is in Christ Jesus would quickly and easily drive away the darkness of this world.

## Spiritual Babylon

Good is the worst enemy of best. There is a gospel, a church, a ministry and a religion which calls itself Christian, but which compels us to feel safe in a spiritual condition in which we remain lost. If the pursuit of happiness and comfort is our primary motivation we will forever be fooled. If we are to respond to our callings and walk in truth, then a commitment to the reality of Romans 12:1 will be required—that we present ourselves as a living and holy sacrifice. A choice is now being presented to us; we can pay now or pay later. To walk in the truth of the gospel will cost us everything now; to not walk in it will cost us everything later.

As a wise proverb states, "Those who forget history are doomed to repeat it." Until now every new move of God has eventually fallen to the same errors made by the previous ones. With all of the emphasis the Scriptures place on learning from the history of God's people it is hard to understand why the church has been so oblivious to the lessons of her own history. The lack of a historical perspective of the church has resulted in her repeating the same devastating mistakes over and over. Without profound changes the next move of God will make a significant spiritual advance only to end in the same kind of disorientation and despair as the previous moves. Before the end the Lord will break this cycle but we must understand it in order to be delivered.

Chapters 17 & 18 of Revelation contain an illumination of "Mystery Babylon." This system is the fruit of the same error having been perpetuated for generation after generation in the church. To properly understand this mystery we must go to its root—the Tower of Babel.

Babylon means "confusion" because it was there that God confused men's languages. James explained, **"For where jealousy and selfish ambition exist, there is disorder (confusion) and every evil thing"** (James 3:16). The building of the tower of Babel is a lucid revelation of the delusion of religious, selfish ambition. This is one of the great manifestations of the same lie started in the garden; that we can be like God without God. The men of Shinar thought they could make it to heaven by their own might and power by building a tower. We may ridicule these men for their incredible delusion but the church has continually tried to do the same thing—to make it to heaven by our own strength.

Building the tower "to heaven" was actually a guise for other motives which they expressed:

> **Come LET US BUILD FOR OURSELVES a city and a tower whose top will reach into heaven, and LET US MAKE A NAME FOR OURSELVES; lest we be scattered abroad over the face of the whole earth (Genesis 11:4).**

After Christianity became the state religion in the third century, to a large degree, politics replaced worship and sacrifice in the ministry. With this change the motives of building for ourselves and making names for ourselves entered and gradually took over as the true vision of the church. Men thought that they could establish the kingdom of God on earth with the sword, crusades, inquisitions and tortures.

It is estimated by historians that over fifty million "heretics," who were in fact true believers who refused to submit to this error, were killed by this beast. She was drunk with the blood of the saints and the true witnesses of Jesus (Revelation 17:6). For over 1,200 years she (the church men had built) ruled over the kings of the earth. She did not take temporal authority but no one else was allowed to without her consent. The Lord looked down upon this abomination and prescribed the same remedy that He did for the first tower— He scattered their languages. Now we have over twenty thousand different languages, or denominations.

## We Who Judge Do the Same Things

This is not to imply that all denominations or organizations are a part of "Mystery Babylon." This is not meant to just point the finger at the Catholic church, but to the church—all of us. The very sins that were committed by the Catholic church in the Middle Ages were also committed by most of the Protestant churches, if only to a lesser scale. While Luther, one of the great prophetic voices of all time, sat composing one of the greatest hymns of all time, *A Mighty Fortress Is Our God,* he was having an Anabaptist starved to death for "heresy."

As Protestants we are repelled by a mere man claiming to be the head of the church, usurping Christ's rightful place, but at the same time we will place almost any charismatic leader on a pedestal to worship. We are repelled by the worship of Mary and the saints but have many of our own idols that we seem no less devoted to. We do need to understand the mistakes of history, and to do this we must look at the Catholic Church *and* the Protestant Church and *our* church. In many cases our sins may be to a lesser degree, but that does not make them any less sins. In some cases our Protestant sins are more hypocritical than the Catholic sins that appear more profane, therefore making our sins more difficult to deal with.

I do not say this in defense of the Catholic Church, but as a fact—it has and still does produce some of the most Christlike men and women on earth. It is true that it has also produced some of the most unchristlike men and women as well. This is also true of the Protestant Church. The enigma is that sometimes this Christlikeness and unchristlike nature is found in the same person! If we are honest with ourselves, we would also have to say the same thing about ourselves. There is a war going on between flesh and spirit that is being waged in every Christian institution and every Christian. The

Lord does not change institutions in order to change people; He changes people in order to change institutions.

When the Scriptures point to the sins of institutions, such as it did in the Book of Revelation, it is so that we can see and repent of the same sins in ourselves. The Book of Revelation was given to John as "a revelation of Jesus Christ" (Revelation 1:1), and yet it seems in this book that most of the revelation is about the man of sin, or Mystery Babylon. This is because the evil natures that are revealed in this book are you and I without Christ. When I point to certain historical facts about an institution it is for this same purpose. We will have no authority to change institutions while we have the same sins in our own lives.

Everything we have built that was really for us, or to make a name for ourselves, is a part of this evil which is about to be destroyed. This is true regardless of how piously we have attached the Lord's name to our diversions. God did not initiate the Tower of Babel project, men did. Self-seeking will always lead us to build that which God is not doing. There is another enemy which attacks that which God is doing and seeks to bring it under the same dominion of selfish ambition—the "control spirit." This spirit tries to take over what God has begun in order to make the work sectarian through pride or fear. The "control spirit" is the most deadly enemy of a true move of God and will continue to be so until the end.

## Great Catholic Revival

In 1992 I was given the understanding that there would be two more significant popes over the Roman Catholic Church. There may be more but I was only shown two, both of which were very significant. The first pope that I saw became enraged against evangelical and charismatic catholics, driving multitudes of them from the church. This pope sought to increase the political prestige and power of the church by intrigue but ultimately brought great humiliation.

After this pope I saw another who was a true lover of God and the whole body of Christ. The spirit of Josiah was upon him to remove idolatry and false doctrines from the church. This man was humble, just and seemingly fearless in his quest to restore the church to Christ. This man will bring such a revival to the Catholic church that it will have an impact on the entire church, which will esteem him as a true brother. He will be cut off at the height of the revival and the whole world will mourn for him. Though I saw these two popes in this sequence I am not certain that their times will come in this order, or if there will not be intervening popes between their reigns.

## Deliverance From Babylon

The call in Revelation 18:4 is to **"Come out of her My people, that you may not participate in her sins and that you may not receive of her plagues."** This call will soon go forth with clarity and power, but He has not called us to come out without leading us to something greater. As a clear revelation of the Mystery Babylon sweeps the body of Christ there will also be a clear revelation of the City Of God.

There will be many in the coming days running around calling everything which is organized "Babylon," causing many to stumble and to miss the purpose of God in their lives. Being free of the babylonian spirit and becoming a part of the City of God is not just a matter of having correct doctrines, but it also includes a deliverance from a wrong heart condition and the receiving of a new heart. Thomas A'Kempis reflected, "What good does it avail a man to be able to discourse profoundly concerning the Trinity, if he is void of humility and thereby displeasing to the Trinity?"

We may want to point the finger and accuse certain denominations for the atrocities of history but if we fall to that we too will miss the point. There are many "non-denominational" churches who are as sectarian and intolerant as any denominational church. Likewise, there are many denominational churches, including some Catholic churches, in which there is little or no sectarian spirit. With which is God pleased?

We are changed by what we are beholding (II Corinthians 3:18). If Babylon has all of our attention we will be changed into its image. If we are beholding the glory of the Lord, we will be changed into that same light, which will itself expose that which is darkness. The destruction of Babylon and her ruler will come **"without human agency"** (Daniel 8:25). As we enter and live in the City of God, judgment on Babylon will be automatic. Leaving Babylon is laying down our self-seeking and the control spirit that causes divisions which separate us from the Lord and each other. Just because we comply with correct doctrines does not mean this has been accomplished. For this reason Paul explained, **"Therefore, from now on we recognize no man [or church] according to the flesh [externals]... "**

This is not to imply that just because we have good intentions when trying to build something for God that it is His work. The "good" of the Tree of Knowledge is just as deadly as the evil; their root is the same. Ministry which is motivated by an attempt to gain God's acceptance is just as much an affront to Him. Jesus paid the price for our acceptance. Anything offered additionally by us to gain His acceptance is a statement that we do not believe His sacrifice was enough to accomplish this. True ministry can only come from a position of *having* God's approval, not trying to acquire it. When Jesus said "It is finished" He was declaring that there was nothing left to be done. JESUS IS the Alpha and Omega, the Beginning and the End of the work of God. We cannot take anything away from or add anything to what He has already accomplished.

*Chapter 8*

# The Finished
# Work of God

This does not mean that because the work is finished we are not to build anything, but the difference is in how we build. We build upon that which is already finished with that which is already finished. The apostle Paul explained:

**For no man can lay a foundation other than the One which is laid, which is JESUS CHRIST. Now if any man builds upon the foundation with gold, silver, precious stones, wood, hay, straw, each man's work will become evident;** *for the day will show it,* **because it is to be revealed with fire; and the fire itself will test the quality of each man's work (I Corinthians 3:11-13).**

Jesus is the foundation, and in a true sense, He is also the entire building—All things are to be summed up in Him. He is the Alpha, the foundation, and he is also the Omega, the Capstone. This was the apostolic message.

Much of what is being called "apostolic" today has already been reduced to a mere emphasis on form, but the true apostolic message gave little or no emphasis to form. The apostles did things to help bring and keep order, such as appointing elders and deacons, but their emphasis was not on form, but formation. They labored that Christ would be formed *IN* the church, not that the church would come into a certain form. This emphasis on form instead of spirit has been the bane and ultimate doom of every move of God since the apostolic age, and it will continue to be so until that which is truly apostolic is raised up again.

There will continue to be ministries raised up, some of whom will actually help to ignite great moves of God, but will also fall to this tendency to believe that the right form for the church can hold and sustain the release of the Spirit. This fallacy will continue to bring many movements to a disappointing stop far short of their potential. One of the same deceptions motivated the men of Shinar—they believed that their new formula or project could keep men from being scattered. *Only* **"In Him (do) all things hold together"** (Colossians 1:17).

Some who will be mightily used of God in the next movements will crash on the same rocks as did the previous movements if this is not understood. Even so, out of this next move there will come those who have a vision for that which is truly apostolic. These will have been delivered from the Babylonian spirit, not just the Babylonian forms, and they will be used to give birth to that which is the true faith of the fathers, the forming of Jesus within. It is **"Christ in us the hope of Glory."**

Every Restoration move until now has ultimately been reduced to the emphasizing of mere doctrine and form. The true apostolic faith will emphasize Life, Himself. Until now we have been content to have the Lord revealed TO us, but a day is coming when He will be revealed IN us. We only need new wineskins if we have new wine. It is a delusion for us to think that merely having a new wineskin can produce the new wine.

In the Book of Revelation, Babylon is visible from the valley, but we must be taken to a "high mountain" to see the New Jerusalem. Deliverance from the Babylonian spirit does

THE FINISHED WORK OF GOD 109

not come just by understanding it. History testifies that many who clearly see and understand this beast are consumed by the same spirit because they do not have a vision of the New Jerusalem. Many of those who preach vehemently against Babylon do so out of the same sectarian spirit. Their preaching inevitably results in a perpetuation of the same Babylonian confusion: more sects who think they alone are right.

## The Ultimate Question

When the first two disciples began to follow Jesus, He challenged them with a question that sooner or later we must all answer: **"What do you seek?"** Their reply was another question, but it was a most appropriate one. **"Lord, where do you dwell?"** They did not ask which sect was the most Scriptural or doctrinally correct, but where is that place that the Lord Himself can abide? This is the only way we can discern the works which are ordained by Him from those that are not—where does the Lord dwell? Not just where does He bless, or even occasionally visit, but where does He *stay*? This is the ultimate apostolic question.

We must distinguish between the things which God blesses and those which He inhabits. Ishmael was a work of the flesh, having been born of the bondwoman and remaining in bondage (Galatians 4:21-31). Ishmael was not the promised seed, but he persecuted the true heir and does so to this day. Yet God blessed him and made him a great nation! He blessed him because of the covenant He had with Abraham, and He often blesses our works of the flesh, to a degree, because of the covenant He has made with us; *however, He will not inhabit them*. The time will come when the child of the flesh must be cast out. We must now look beyond that which may have a blessing upon it and give our attention to that which He inhabits.

Ishmael was allowed to remain in the house of Abraham until he began to mock and persecute Isaac. This is the separation point which begins to distinguish the works that originate in the flesh and those that are born of the promise; those which are born of the flesh sooner or later will not be able to resist accusing and attacking the works which they feel have encroached on their territory. Isaac did not have to attack Ishmael because he knew who he was and was not threatened by Ishmael. The works of the flesh are not so secure. These will often do their attacking under the veil of protecting the truth as watchmen for the church, but the true motivation is always territorial preservation.

## Strong Delusions

For nearly two thousand years the Lord has been working to prepare His church for this hour. Satan has likewise been earnestly working to deceive and side-track every purpose of God in the church. One of Satan's most effective strategies has been to get the church to worship the things of God in place of God. He has succeeded in getting the church to worship the church, the Bible, even to worship in place of God Himself. One of his most effective delusions has been to get us to devote our attention to who we are in Christ, instead of who He is in us. This leads to the worshipping of ourselves, the creature, instead of the blessed Creator.

Of course, it is important that we know who we are in Christ, but this must never be exalted or emphasized above who He is in us. Almost all distractions involve truths that are from God, but we have worshipped the gifts in place of the Giver. The church is called to be the bride of the Lamb; she is most dear to the heart of God, but what groom would be pleased with a bride who was more consumed with her own beauty and person than she was with him? Such self-centeredness would be repulsive.

The Bible is a gift of immeasurable value, but it is not knowing the book of the Lord that should be our goal, but knowing the Lord of the book. We were created for God's pleasure and true worship is probably the highest state of fulfillment that we can know in this life. However it has become easy for us to become infatuated with the state of fulfillment that we receive even more than we are with the One we are worshipping.

Regardless of our pretense, we are worshipping that which has our attention. Satan knows we will never become "who we are in Christ" as long as that is our motivation. We will only become who we are called to be when Jesus and His glory are the focus of our attention. We will be changed only by seeing His glory, not our own (as if we had any of our own). This deception of getting us to concentrate on who we are instead of who He is, has sidetracked and led into extremes many of the truths restored in preparation for this hour. But this delusion will not prevail; the glory of the Lord will dispel it like a wisp of smoke before a great wind.

The latter glory of the Lord's house will be greater than the former house, but this does not mean that the house itself is greater. It is the glory which fills the house, the presence of the Lord, that is greater. When the glory fills the temple it is not the temple that gets the attention. Those who do attain to all that He has called them to will probably not even be aware of it; their attention will not be on what they have attained, but on pleasing the One who sent them. The believers who walk in the fullness of what is to come will not be focused on serving the temple of the Lord, but on serving the Lord of the temple. The church, ministry, spiritual truths, or even the Bible can become idols when they become the *focus* of our attention. Those who overcome and fulfill their callings do so by following the Lamb wherever He goes. Then all of the wonderful gifts and callings of God take their rightful place and become aids instead of distractions.

The delusions of self-centeredness and self-worship that now permeate the church and much of our teaching will be broken. The Lord Himself is about to enter His temple, and all crowns will be cast at His feet. Those who have presumed positions of leadership without commission will be evident. Everyone who has exalted himself will be humbled. Those who have humbled themselves will be anointed and commissioned. This army now being formed will be greater than anything ever seen or dreamed of, but this army will not be magnifying itself; it will magnify the King who leads it.

Those who perform the greatest works will be taking little notice of their own accomplishments. They will not esteem themselves highly, not because of insecurity, but because of their recognition of the One who works through them and what He has accomplished. These will not be measuring themselves by others, but by Him. Just as the Queen of Sheba was speechless before Solomon's wisdom and the glory of his kingdom, those who have seen Jesus are even far more so before Him. Those who have truly seen the Lord will, like Him, flee to the mountains when men try to make them kings or exalt them in any way. Their authority will not come through man; it will come from above.

## The Danger of Authority

During this harvest human authority and institutions will be melting like wax. As the masses will be seeking anyone to take authority during these times, this comes as a warning! There will be doctrines promulgated encouraging believers to seek authority through institutional and political means. The Lord's kingdom is not of this world and His kingdom will not come through this present world's systems. The enemy will use these doctrines to attract those who are self-seeking and self-promoting. Those with such motives will not have leadership in this harvest. The authority the Lord will establish is different from what even His own people now perceive. We must not try to rule, but to serve. Through this His authority will flow and begin to bring order though Peace.

Twentieth century Christianity has become quite adept at converting men from the evil side of the Tree Of Knowledge while not dealing with the "good" side of the same tree, which is just as deadly and far more deceptive. In Israel, some of the most evil, and even the demon possessed, bowed the knee to Jesus. It was the most upstanding citizens who crucified Him. Man's goodness is offered as a compensation for righteousness and is therefore an affront and an enemy to the cross. When we try to stand on our own good works it is a statement that we do not think we need the propitiation made for us by Jesus. Man's goodness is as filthy rags in the sight of God and is a far more formidable enemy to the gospel than the evil side of that tree. It will be those who are eating from the "good" of the Tree of Knowledge who bring the greatest persecution against the advancing church. It will be the "good" fruit from the Tree of Knowledge which deceives and causes more to stumble than the manifest evil of these times.

## The Redemption Business

Some of the ministries who will bring the greatest life to the church in the days to come will be those who have made the great mistakes in the past. It is a Biblical and historical reality that many fail so totally that they come to the end of all human effort and strength before God will use them. Humility comes before exaltation.

We see this precedent in the life of the patriarchs. Abraham brought forth an Ishmael before the Isaac. Joseph saw the sun and moon and stars bowing to him, but first he had to become a slave and then a prisoner. Moses tried to deliver his brethren by his own strength and had to spend forty years in the wilderness as a shepherd, the most humble profession of the times, before God could use him. David, after being anointed as the next king, spent years as a fugitive hiding from the very people he was called to rule. Peter had to deny the Lord before he could be used as one of His greatest witnesses. Paul had to become the chief of sinners persecuting the church unto death before he could be the "apostle of grace." This may not be true for all, but it seems to be for those who would be used for the greatest spiritual advances. Many of the elders and early church fathers would put little trust in anyone who had not been broken by such failure or discipline.

From the third chapter of Genesis to the end, the Bible deals with one essential theme—redemption. In a sense we might say that God is in the redemption business; it is His heart to recover and restore what has been lost. Because of this, many of the individuals involved in terrible spiritual failures will become even more useful to the Lord because of those failures, and He will restore them and use them mightily. The humility caused by these failures will enable the Lord to entrust them with even more spiritual authority, just like He did Peter after his denial.

Nevertheless, we must understand the failures or we will be doomed to repeat them. We must also know that just understanding the problems of the past will not keep us from repeating them. Hearts must be changed by repentance and by seeing the Lord's glory more clearly; we must both STOP eating of the Tree of Knowledge and START eating of the Tree of Life. Just doing one without the other will not accomplish our deliverance.

## Knowledge vs. Life

In the sixties and seventies many great truths were restored to the church. Though some of these were timely and needed, they were carried to extremes and used to derail a renewal, leading much of the church into stagnation and disorientation.

This was usually due to a misapplication of a teaching rather than error in the teaching itself. Even correct doctrine will be carried to extremes when it becomes an end instead of a means. This produces overreactions in which can easily cause just as much damage as the extremes.

The early church had encounters with God, and then wrote about them. Since then many have been trying to write about them and then have the encounter, often substituting having a correct concept of the truth in place of the encounter with God. This has resulted in having a form of godliness without God.

For example, how many, after studying the community of the early church, duplicated everything they did in order to effect the same spirit and commitment to church life, only to have it result in another dead form? The early church did not have community because they did things in a certain way but because God was moving in their midst. When God is moving His people want to be joined together and will do so without pressure. When God is moving truth becomes life. If He is not moving, all of our formulas, principles and attempts to get the people motivated will be counterproductive.

Christianity is not just a system of truths and principles, it is a relationship with a living God. Truths and principles instituted before the relationship is established are still rooted in the Tree of Knowledge—regardless of how accurate the truths may be death will be their ultimate fruit. Only when the relationship is established are we safe to implement truths and principles.

The Lord never said we would know those who were His because all of their doctrines were accurate. There is only one way to discern those who are true servants: *by their fruit.* Of course, all who love the truth will want their doctrines to be accurate, but it is better to have some wrong doctrines or concepts but be humble before the Lord than to have right doctrines with pride. Those who are wrong but have humility can be corrected. Those who are right but proud usually end up doing more damage to the church and the cause of Christ than many false teachers. Our goal must be to have right doctrines, but with humility and an entreatable, tolerant spirit that loves even those who are in error just as our Lord does.

Consider the doctrine of submission to authority. This was a timely truth for the body of Christ when it became an emphasis in the late sixties. The world and the church were suffering a terrible onslaught of lawlessness and disorientation. But much of the application of this truth actually brought about fruit that was contrary to the very doctrine itself. Many of the most humble and submissive men and women of God were blackballed from ministry because they did not comply with certain people's doctrine of submission. At the same time some of the most arrogant and rebellious individuals were released and promoted in the church because they complied with, or at least could verbally articulate, the doctrine of submission. Which is preferable, having a correct doctrine on submission or being submissive? The truth that God requires is not in the minds but in the hearts.

There have been "lone rangers" causing confusion in the body of Christ, but all of the lone rangers combined hardly caused the discord and confusion of the few who overemphasized submission. Nowhere does the Scripture warn us to beware of those who are not submitted to the body; the warning is to beware of those who are not joined to the Head. According to many popular doctrines of submission one can be "properly" joined to the body without even being joined to the Head, and many are. But if we are truly joined to the Head we will be properly joined to the body also, though it may not be in a way that complies with our doctrine or meets our approval.

## Being Properly Joined

The issue is not whether or not we should be joined to the body properly, but how it is to be accomplished. The church is not an end but a means. The end of all things is to be summed up in Christ. The whole purpose of God for His people is that they be conformed to the image of His Son. We do not become the church in order to do this; we become the church *when* we have done this. The church is *not* the pattern for the church; *Jesus is the pattern for the church*. Every time we get beguiled from the simplicity of devotion to Christ, not the church, nor a doctrine, and not even to His servants but devotion to the Lord Himself, we lose our way.

When a major televangelist confessed his sins publicly, he made the statement that he did not really have a single friend that he could be open and share his problems with. This statement was taken by many as *the* reason for his problems. Though he had so many people around him and seemed to have conformed to all of the principles of submission to the body, he was obviously not truly submitted. Even so, his failure to be submitted to the church was not the problem, but just a symptom of a much deeper problem, one that all will face who arc given to majoring on minors.

In some of the councils of elders and leaders with the very highest standards of mutual accountability and submission, recent scandals have uncovered immorality and homosexuality among members that had been going on for years. This alone should wake us up to the fact that something has been seriously wrong with our concept of submission. The moral, ethical, and heretical problems arising from the church are not because there is not enough submission to the body but because there is not enough submission to the Head. We can fool our most intimate associates, our families, and even the press, but we cannot fool God. The problems that have been surfacing in the church are because of a lack of the true and holy fear of the Lord, which is the essence of true submission. The answer to this is not to throw out our submission to one another, but to give even greater emphasis to that which is more important—our submission to the Lord. Only then will our submission to each other be real.

## Touching God's Heart

The reducing of truth from the Person to a mere doctrine has led to the distortion of every truth restored over the last few centuries. When Martha approached Jesus after the death of her brother, He told her that Lazarus would rise again. She said she knew he would rise on the last day. Her faith was in the doctrine of the resurrection, not in Him. He redirected her faith, saying, "I am the Resurrection." Jesus is not only the resurrection, he is all truth.

It is possible to have all of our doctrines in perfect order without having life. It is also possible to have life in Jesus before we have all of our doctrines in perfect order. We see a good example of this in Martha and Mary. When Martha declared that had Jesus been there her brother would not have died, she got a real good teaching about the resurrection. When her sister Mary came out and asked *the identical question* Jesus wept, ***"being deeply moved in spirit,"*** and then He raised Lazarus from the dead.

Martha got a good teaching about the resurrection; Mary got a resurrection! That's because Mary had a relationship with Jesus that could move Him "deeply in spirit". Even though Mary was just as wrong in her understanding as Martha, Mary could move God Himself deeply; she could cause God Himself to weep. Mary *had* chosen the "best part."

Jesus is Truth, and those who love Him love truth. We do want our understanding to be accurate, but having our facts right is not as important as our relationship to Him. If our relationship to Him is not right, having all doctrines laid out properly is still eating from the Tree of Knowledge, and it will still bring death.

## True Faith

In spite of the considerable emphasis on faith for the last two decades, the true substance of faith continues to elude most of the church. This emphasis was timely, the church desperately needs more faith to accomplish the purposes of God for this hour, but faith is not mere principles and formulas. Often we have substituted a faith in one's faith for true faith in God.

True faith is simply the recognition of the One in whom we believe. Jesus is not only the Resurrection, He is Faith, and He is every Truth. He is "I AM." That's why Paul declared, **"For as many as may be the promises of God,** *in Him* **they are yes"** (II Corinthians 1:20). He further testified of this to the Galatians: **"Now the promises were spoken to Abraham and to his seed. He does not say, 'and to his seeds,' as referring to many,** *but rather to One,* **'and to your Seed,'** *that is Christ"* (Galatians 3:16). The promises of God are not given to us independently of Him, but IN Him. The promises were not given to be consumed by our selfish desires, they were given for His glory. To get us to use the promises of God for selfish reasons has been one of Satan's most effective temptations, so successful that he even tried to use it on Jesus.

Some have carried these doctrines to an even more dangerous extreme; presuming to use God's authority *on Him*! This is what cost Moses his own inheritance in the promised land. He was told once to strike the Rock, which was a type of Christ Who was to be struck *once* (see I Corinthians 10:4). The next time he was to bring water from the Rock he was directed to "speak to the Rock." This was to symbolize that once Christ was struck all we would have to do was to speak to Him and the living waters would flow. But Moses allowed his frustration with the people to drive him to strike the Rock again using the rod that God had given him. The rod speaks of the authority God does give to us but we are not to use it to strike Him with it. Such presumption can likewise cost us our inheritance.

Every truth will be carried to extremes by some. Others, because of the extremes, reject the truth altogether, or swing back to the opposite extreme. Both can miss the purpose of God, but those who carry truth to extremes are usually corrected and learn valuable lessons from their mistakes. Those who sit in judgment and overreact in fear of error often become like the dwarfs in C.S. Lewis' *The Last Battle*. The battle was over and Aslan, who was the Christ figure, came to let them out of their dreary hiding place. But they refused to come out! They were so sure that He was just another deceiver that they could not be delivered from their darkness. Some are so afraid of being "taken in" that they cannot be taken out of their bondage. Those who are the most fearful of error are the most difficult to lead out into light and they usually spend their lives in a most dreary place. The fear of deception will not keep us from deception; it will lead to our deception. The only thing which will keep us from being deceived is a love for the Truth, Himself.

No one wants to make mistakes. It would be a terrible thing to be responsible for injuring a neighbor's child—how much more grievous is it to cause one of the Lord's children to stumble? As James warned us, teaching is a serious matter: **"Let not many of you become teachers, my brethren, knowing that as such we shall incur a stricter judgment"** (James 3:1). The worst offense in Scripture that of being a stumbling block. The judgment soon to come upon the household of God will be even more intense upon the teachers. If we are wise teachers we will pray for it. His judgment is for our salvation, not for condemnation. It is better to receive the discipline of the Lord than to lead even one of His little ones astray.

After the judgment that the Lord is bringing upon His household first, there will not be as many teachers. Teaching in His name will be seen as the holy and serious matter that it is. The teachers who are left will not be given just to the elaboration of mere facts and principles, but to the impartation of a love for the Truth. As an old proverb explains, "If you give a man a fish he has one meal. If you teach him how to fish he can feed himself for the rest of his life." Those who are taught about God are never satisfied. Those who are taught to love God and seek Him for themselves will have a river of living water flowing out of their own innermost being.

## Chapter 9

# Saul Comes
# Before David

With almost every new move of the Spirit there is often a premature movement attempted by the church in the same area. We might say that there is usually a "Saul" before there is a "David." This principle includes ministries, movements and restored truths. When we see truths like submission, discipleship, faith and others, become emphases, and then get carried to extremes, we must understand that this is sometimes because God is about to speak concerning the same issues. There is a degree of submission He will require in the days to come which exceeds the present comprehension of most of the church. There is a true discipleship that we need in this hour like never before. There is to be a faith required in the days to come which greatly exceeds that which we presently know. We must not be driven to overreaction because some have carried these truths to extremes.

King Saul was anointed by God and he did accomplish some of the purposes of God. Many of Saul's devoted followers did, in time, recognize David and joined his company to become honored associates. Many who may have been in the service of what could be recognized as "Saul" were men of faith and courage who pushed beyond the established limits of their time. Their work may have ultimately been sidetracked, but in some ways it can help prepare the way for that which we might call "David"—the symbol of God's provision. Of course these premature movements can also make it more difficult for God's provision to be recognized, just as it took the men of Israel a few years to be able to receive another king after the debacle with Saul. However, even this will ultimately work for the purpose of God.

Saul was crowned because the men of Israel started to feel the need for a king. They felt the need for a king because the Lord had put that need in their hearts as He was preparing them for the king He had promised, the one whose lineage would be from the tribe of Judah and who would reign until Shiloh (Jesus) came (Genesis 49:10). Samuel was raised up as a prophet to prepare Israel for this king and to anoint him. But Israel could not wait for God's provision just as Abraham could not wait for Isaac. Saul was man's king not God's. God's king was not yet mature enough to take authority. We can get sidetracked with "present truth" in the same way. We begin to see the truth, we know it is needed, so we move out to establish it before the proper time, or before it is mature enough.

Israel's impatience cost them. After Saul, it took them a long time to accept God's true king. So it is with almost every truth the Lord restores to the church. Seldom have men been able to wait for God's provision before going on to formulate that which is merely the result of our own human striving. Man's provision must always die before God's provision can take its place. David moved to Hebron and was accepted as the king by the tribe of Judah seven years before the rest of the nation would accept him. Likewise, God's provision is usually accepted only by a portion of the church for a period before the whole church can forget the extremes of the past and come in fully to the purpose of God. We see this cycle prevalent throughout church history.

Even in the days of Saul's reign there were some who recognized David as the Lord's king. These joined him in the cave of obscurity and humility. Just as David was prepared for his calling and authority by his rejection, humiliation and tribulations, so the truths of God are purified in those who receive them and hold to them in spite of the fire's testing. We must not despise this time of preparation, but embrace it and make the most of it.

Those who joined themselves to David in the cave were misfits in Israel, as is often true with those who are first to receive God's truths. But the caves transformed them along with David; some of these men became the greatest warriors and most faithful leaders in David's reign. The great truths which have transformed the church and changed the course of history have seldom come out of the ivory towers of esoteric theological discourse. The vessels of prophetic truth have almost always been the obscure spiritual misfits who live in spiritual caves and holes in the ground. This will continue to be true until the end.

We need not be discouraged by the doctrines or movements which seem to confuse the body of Christ. When the doctrines of men rise to create such havoc, we can take courage that God's truth in the matter has already been born and will mature until the proper time for its revelation. The different "Sauls" will just help us to appreciate the "Davids" that much more. There is true revelation from God coming on faith, discipleship, spiritual authority, the kingdom, and unity, as well as many other doctrines which may now be causing a disruption in the body of Christ. We must not be too quick to follow the first movement or new teaching which seems to be head and shoulders above the rest. When such a doctrine arises start looking for the young shepherds faithfully tending their little flocks, or the little bands of misfits hiding in caves. That is where we will usually find God's provision until Saul is dead.

It is natural to wonder why Saul was anointed as king by the Lord. Why did He give into the people's impatience? Because of God's covenant with us He will bless our works as much as He can, even works that originate from our own impatience, like Ishmael, the son born after the flesh. The Lord blessed and made Ishmael a great nation, because of Abraham. The Lord is faithful even when we are unfaithful. But if we want to be a part of the promised seed, truth, or ministry, we must distinguish between that which is blessed by God and that which is *chosen*. **"Many are called but few are chosen"** (Matthew 22:14). There are many ministries today which are anointed and blessed but are still works of the flesh, having their origin in the mind and striving of men, not in the heart of God. Like Saul, they may lead the church for a time but they will soon pass into oblivion. While Saul enjoyed the blessing and following of the people, David appeared cursed, and so it usually is until the appointed time.

## The Test

One of the great tests of David's heart was his willingness to serve in the house of Saul. He slew the giant Goliath and fought in his battles. David did not return evil for evil but good for evil, just as the coming Messiah who would one day sit on the throne of David, a throne that had to be established with such great character. David obviously viewed the overall well-being of Israel and the purposes of God as more important than his own well-being or recognition. This is in some way a test required of all who would serve the eternal throne of David upon which Christ now sits.

Saul could not long endure God's chosen heir to his throne just as Ishmael could not endure Isaac and taunted him. There is enmity between that which is born of the flesh and that which is born of the spirit. Saul continually tried to kill David but David would not raise his hand against Saul. He would not take the authority for himself but waited patiently even during intense persecution and injustice for God to establish him in His time. Retaliation and self-promotion will not be found in that which is truly born of God. Those who allow "Saul" to antagonize them into retaliation or self-promotion will find themselves disqualified from leadership in God's chosen ministry.

There is a single great distinguishing characteristic between Saul and David that can be found as the primary characteristic that separates almost every work that is born of the flesh from that which is born of God. When Saul observed the people scattering and the enemies gathering, he performed the sacrifice even though he had been commanded to wait. He did this because he feared the people and the circumstances more than he feared God. When pressed by what must have been one of the greatest trials a man could endure, having his family kidnapped as well as those of all his faithful men, David would not do anything until he had inquired of the Lord, even when his own men threatened to stone him. David feared the Lord more than men or circumstances. Such is the nature of true spiritual authority. Such is the nature of those who have been chosen for leadership during the greatest move of God the earth has ever witnessed. One of the ultimate tests of leadership will come in who we fear the most, men or God.

Not only was David the youngest son in the insignificant house of Jesse, he was a shepherd, the most humble profession of his day. In the natural, there was nothing in the life of David that would indicate his high calling. It had to be that way. For the kingdom to be built on righteousness it could not be one that attracted those who were drawn by appearances or who saw prosperity in that which is carnal and temporary. The only ones who would recognize David were those who saw both greatness and prosperity in that which is of the heart, those who loved the truth more than anything this world could give them. It was for this same reason that Jesus was born in a stable.

## God Was Born in a Stable

In Biblical times the stable was a most offensive place. The floors were composed of impacted dung and other filth which had accumulated for decades. The stench was so great they were placed as far away from other dwellings as possible. By today's standards they would not even be fit for animals. That the Lord of Glory would choose such a place to make His entry into this world is one of the more profound revelations of His message to man. We would do well not to miss His point as He has not ceased to use such places to make His appearances.

Human reasoning would never lead us to a stable to find God. The only way He could be found was by revelation; only those who were led by the Spirit would come. This has not changed. That which has been born of God is usually found in a place that is repulsive to the pride and presumptions of carnal men. As the apostle stated it, "… **God has chosen the foolish things of the world to shame the wise, and God has chosen the weak things of the world to shame the things which are strong, and the base things of the world and the despised, God has chosen, the things that are not, that He might nullify the things that are, that no man should boast before God**" (I Corinthians 1:27-29).

After His birth Jesus was then raised in the most despised town in the nation. Even His physical appearance was such that no one would be attracted to Him (Isaiah 53:2). He left this world after the most degrading torture and execution yet devised by the base and demented schemes of fallen men. This gospel is foolishness to the natural man and always will be. It will never attract those who live by human wisdom.

Only those who love truth more than anything else in this world will walk with Him in the reproach of the true gospel.

The birth, life and death of Jesus put the ax to the root of the tree of human wisdom and pride, which is the fruit of the Tree of Knowledge of Good and Evil. It is the most powerful message the creation has ever heard; it is the most profound testimony of the character and nature of God. When we embellish this gospel to make it appeal to carnal men, we destroy its power to set them free and we ourselves begin to drift from the path of life. For this reason Paul preached nothing but Christ and Him crucified. He knew that if one were compelled to come by any other message it would be a false conversion.

## False Conversions

This is a reason for much of the powerlessness of the church today; we have converted men to the church, to our doctrines, to our projects and organizations—to almost anything but Christ Himself. We do this because the true gospel seems too offensive. We feel that the raw truth of the gospel is doomed to be rejected as foolishness, which is precisely the very power of its message. It is *meant* to be rejected by those who do not love the truth more than their pride. The gospel is meant to be rejected by those who would tend to use it for self-promotion and the approval of men.

A man may gain fame throughout the world, do many miracles and cast out many devils, only to come before the Lord and hear that He never knew them. If we would preach only the raw gospel we would be protecting the church from the terrible deceptions and humiliations she has been enduring for almost two millenniums. We would also be protecting the deceivers from a life of delusion in which they believe they are really serving God, that they would not have to hear those terrible words from the Lord on that day, "Depart from

Me. I never knew you." Many of the deceivers might have entered into a true salvation had we been faithful not to compromise the gospel.

If we are to be true ministers we must heed the apostle's word: **"Have this attitude in yourself which was also in Christ Jesus, who, although He existed in the form of God did not regard equality with God a thing to be grasped, but** *emptied* **Himself, taking the form of a bondservant... He** *humbled Himself*, **becoming obedient to the point of death, even death on the cross"** (Philippians 2:5-48).

Upon entering ministry Jesus emptied Himself and became of no reputation. When we enter ministry with the intention of being filled and making a reputation, we have made a fundamental departure from true ministry. To repeat a most important exhortation for us all: **"He who speaks from himself seeks his own glory [or recognition]; but he who is seeking the glory of the one who sent him, he is true"** (John 7:18).

The revelations and shakings in some of the large visible ministries have more purpose than just getting our eyes off of men and back onto the Lord, (though that is important). We have often been preaching a false gospel. It does not matter how tearfully someone talks about the cross, if we are not living it, it is not in our message. Self promotion was the original temptation and it is still one of the most effective in rendering the church and its gospel powerless in bringing about true conversion and true rebirth. The false gospel will swell our church rolls and inflate our donations but is repulsive to God as He warned: **"You are those who justify yourselves in the sight of men, but God knows your hearts; for that which is highly esteemed among men is detestable in the sight of God"** (Luke 16:15).

That the world is now laughing and scorning the visible church is a just retribution; we must reap what we sow. We wanted the world's recognition and now it has judged us rightly. But there is an invisible church which does not seek the world's recognition or approval. As prophesied, this church has been protected and nourished by God in the wilderness of obscurity (Revelation 12:1-6). It has no name or earthly organization. Most of its members do not even understand it; they have wandered about in spiritual caves and holes in the ground. They are sojourners who could not be satisfied with the cities built by men build; they keep looking for the one that God has built. Some are true shepherds, some are true wisemen, by revelation they are being led to the stables where the True One is being brought forth once again.

In some of the most humble works and ministries the God of glory has chosen to bring forth powerful men and women of the faith. To some of the most meek and humble servants a sword has been given that will soon bring to an end the futile works of unbroken religious impostors. Then they will shake the entire world with the true gospel of the kingdom. The whole world is about to understand that He does resist the proud, but He gives grace to the humble.

To see the Lord's true work we must often go to places that require the death of our flesh and sometimes our reputations. We must also have the heart of Simeon and Anna, who could see in a mere infant the salvation of the world. Don't be discouraged if you don't yet see the fruit; look for the seed that will become the fruit. This does not mean that He is only found in the poor, the wretched and the despised, but that is where He is usually found.

Again there stands One among us who very few really know. He is growing in individuals and works that we would never suspect without a revelation. Those who find Him will no longer care about being known or accepted by men—they will only want to be known by Him. In Him are found all of the treasures of wisdom and knowledge. The knowledge of

Him is more valuable than all of the earth's riches. When we know Him all of the wealth and pomp of men seems pitiful.

The true gospel will never appeal to the carnal nature of man: it will confront that nature and put the ax to its root. As Paul declared, **"If I were still trying to please men I would not be a bond-servant of Christ"** (Galatians 1:10). We must make a choice as to whom we are going to serve. It will be Christ or mammon, but it will never be both.

## We Will Know Them by Their Fruit

Jesus came as a humble carpenter from the most humble town in the most despised nation on earth. Most of those who were called to preach His gospel were "untrained and untaught." This has never changed, and it will not be changed until the end. The Lord is about to correct the church's tendency to know men according to their credentials, which seminary or Bible school they attended, or even by who laid hands on them, instead of by their fruit. This deception has led to a great portion of the error and darkness which still dominates the church. The Lord warned us against such foolishness and His ways from the beginning have been a witness against it.

Those who continue in this error of judging by credentials will be deceived and will become deceivers. Those who do not repent of this will reject those the Lord sends and approve of those He has not sent. From now on we must recognize no man according to the flesh (externals) but according to the spirit. In the days to come the only way we will be able to recognize those who are true messengers will be according to Acts 4:13: **"Now as they [the Sanhedrin] observed the confidence of Peter and John, and understood that they were uneducated and untrained men, they were marveling, and began to recognize them** *as having been with Jesus."*

These are the only truly reliable credentials—the presence of the Lord in a person's life. Degrees from schools, experience, even their ability to expound the Scriptures accurately and articulately, can be helpful, but should never be the only basis upon which we accept or approve someone. The issue is—have they been with Jesus? Are they ministering Jesus or that which may be true but is in fact the fruit of the Tree of Knowledge?

The Lord's determination to send those who are unacceptable according to the world's standards is a judgment against the world's pride and rebellion; this is the same pride and rebellion that caused the fall of man and is bringing judgment upon the entire earth. If the church does not repent of this she will partake of the world's judgment in this. Even the great apostle Paul, who was learned and trained, was displayed in "weakness, and in fear and much trembling" (I Corinthians 2:3). As he told the Galatians, his flesh was a trial to them, yet they received him as an angel (messenger) of God (see Galatians 4:14). If we are going to receive the truth and the true ones, we have got to see beyond externals, to love the truth more than our pride, and to love and openly accept the humble, because God **"resists the proud but gives grace to the humble"** (James 4:6).

The day is upon us when the Lord will have no more mercy on pride and human presumption. This judgment, like all judgments, will begin with His own household. He is once again crying over His own people: **"O Jerusalem, Jerusalem, who kills the prophets and stones those who are sent to her! How often I wanted to gather your children together, the way a hen gathers her chicks under her wings, and you were unwilling. Behold, your house is being left to you desolate! For I say to you,** *from now on you shall not see Me until you say, 'blessed is He who comes in the name of the Lord!'"* (Matthew 23:37-39)

We will not see Him again until we see Him in those whom He sends. The church is just as guilty now as Jerusalem was then. Time after time He tried to gather us together and we stoned those He sent to help us. But there is soon to be a people who will not judge by what their eyes see. These will know no man according to externals but after the Spirit. These will recognize Him and receive Him, in everyone in whom He dwells. As a result they will be gathered under His wings and protected from the onslaught to come.

The only Biblical protection against deluding influences is to have a love for the Truth. Only those who keep their first love will escape deception in these times. If we have any other motive for following Him we will be in jeopardy. Selfish ambition, fear of hell, the need to be identified with a strong social entity, idealism, the need to please others, love for the excitement and miracles, seeking God's provision, or any other reason will prove to be inadequate foundations for our faith.

## The Deceptions Never Change

Almost every deception is rooted in the original lie the serpent used to deceive Eve—that we can become like God without God. Delusions will turn the focus of our attention upon ourselves, just as they did when our first parents ate of that deadly fruit and then looked at themselves. These things have not changed from the beginning.

Most delusions will be based on an element of truth. Satan still comes as an "angel of light" or "messenger of truth". Just because something is true does not mean that it is life. The "good" side of the Tree of Knowledge looks good because it IS good, but human goodness is motivated by self-righteousness and self-promotion. For this reason the "Pharisee of Pharisees" who was "according to the Law, found blameless," persecuted the Way unto death. As the Lord Himself testified, the publicans and harlots will enter the kingdom before the upstanding citizens who are self-righteous.

Because delusions can be based in truth, we will not always be able to identify them merely by their compliance with Scripture. Satan quotes Scripture to deceive, just as he did to Jesus. We can judge only by the fruit. Where does the teaching focus our attention? Does it glorify the Lord or men? Regardless of how often and how emotionally we may use His name, selfish ambition is still selfish ambition, and it will inevitably lead to deception.

In the days to come there will be men performing miracles and demonstrating great power in order to testify of and verify their ministries, just as there have been for many years. There is another kind of minister coming who will perform even greater works but will not even care to have people know who he is. Publicity will be a burden to this new breed of minister, not a thrill. They will not seek attention for themselves, or their ministries, but for the One who sent them. These are true messengers. These will have no desire for building great organizations but rather with building great people, which has been the heart of God from the beginning. Like Abraham, those who see the city which God is building out of living stones will not be distracted by the projects contrived by men.

When the fire of tribulation comes it will not be our discipline, our submission, or even our knowledge of the truth that keeps us faithful; the only thing that will keep us is the grace of God that will be manifested by a love for Truth, Himself. This cannot be overemphasized. In the end, everyone will quit except for those in love. When our love grows cold, that is when we drift. If we are giving ourselves to seek anything in this day it should be the Father's love for the Son, and the Son's love for the Father. This must be the complete focus of our attention. If we do not see and hold in our vision the central purpose of God to sum up all things *in* His Son we will always be in danger of being consumed by the lesser purposes of God, or even worse distractions.

As the apostle Paul explained, in what may be the greatest summation of true apostolic vision: **"*One thing* I do; forgetting what lies behind and reaching forward to what lies ahead, I press on toward the goal for the prize of the high calling of God in Christ Jesus" (Philippians 3:13-14)**. Jesus *is* the high calling of God. Being found in Him is our purpose. This statement may be the fundamental issue which separates true apostles from pretenders; the true apostle keeps his vision focused on the "one thing," the Father's love for His Son and presenting all men complete in Him.

When we are concentrated upon the primary purpose of God the secondary purposes will all then serve the one. If our eye is single, on Him, then the whole body will be full of light. If our eye is not single but divided into the many secondary purposes, it will become darkness instead of light. Even though they may be truths they will still deceive us; they will become distorted and extreme if our focus is not on the Lord Himself. Deception is not just misunderstanding truth, it is not being in His will, it is not doing what He called us to do, which is first and foremost, to abide in Him. Only when we have a love for the truth do we believe in our hearts and not just with our heads. It is those who believe in their hearts who shall be saved.

## A Coming Emphasis in the Church

A coming emphasis in the church will be humility. But humility, like submission, is not always what it appears to be. Saul was "small in his own eyes," but is a man really humble if he can make a decision which will affect thousands of the Lord's own children without even consulting Him? What appeared to be humility was really insecurity. Those who are insecure tend to swing to the other extreme of presumption, often in overreaction to circumstances and fears. Still, the Lord said that He could use Saul as long as he was small in his own eyes as this is certainly better than pride or presumption. Insecurity must be replaced by a true security in the Lord or we will be continually in jeopardy of falling to carnal authority.

Insecurity mixed with authority has led to some of the most presumptuous acts in history. Despots have killed millions out of perverted self preservation. Insecurity caused Saul to slay the Lord's own priests and to try to kill David. True humility is not insecurity; true humility it is simply understanding who God is. Insecurity is still the fruit of the Tree of Knowledge; it has our attention on ourselves. True humility has its attention on God.

Pride will lead to a fall and the Lord resists the proud, but if we start judging who is proud and who is humble according to a doctrine we ourselves have fallen to pride, and will almost certainly find ourselves judging the Lord's chosen and receiving those who walk in carnal authority. Even the great prophet Samuel was prone to this error. One would think that after the failure of Saul he would not again judge after the flesh. But upon going to the house of Jesse to anoint God's chosen vessel he immediately thought that the son who was the most physically imposing was the one. He was mistaken, and so are we time after time because of the same inclination.

We should not be overly awed by many of the knowledgeable, articulate and dynamic performers and speakers who draw great crowds, but rather be praying for them. Even if we draw multitudes and have great success in our ministry by fulfilling the purposes of God, we will be the most vulnerable when enjoying success and human approval. As the wise apostle exhorted, **"Take heed when you think you stand, lest you fall"** (I Corinthians 10:12).

It is easier to require truth from someone than to require life from them. It is easy to know all about the Lord and still not know Him. We may know all about Him but still be "worshipping an unknown God." Just having right doctrines will not deliver us from the fire that is coming. Neither will have the approval or following of great numbers—we must know Jesus as our Life.

*Chapter 10*

# The Persecution

Before the great ingathering Christianity will experience a great humiliation. The enemy's strategy is to so utterly degrade the church that she will begin to retreat just when she is about to make one of her greatest advances. The "accuser of the brethren" will go forth with unprecedented rage against the Body of Christ. The "revelations" of immoral and unethical behavior by hundreds of highly visible ministries will bring about a loathing of Christianity throughout the world, for *a time*. These "revelations" will include child molesting, rape, and the most vile forms of perversion. Some of these will be true, but *most will not be true.*

## The Need for Discernment

There has never been a more critical need for the church to have the gift of discernment of spirits. In many cases, even when all of the evidence appears irrefutable, there will be entrapment and the accused will be innocent. Some of those who will appear as champions of righteousness by exposing others in order to "cleanse the temple" will be deceivers themselves who actually will have helped to set up the entrapments, or to have brought fabrications against Christian leaders. We must know each other after the Spirit, not rumors, or sometimes what even appears to be hard evidence.

Satan's hit list includes hundreds of Christian leaders. It will target some who have recently made mistakes which were publicly exposed, but the new charges will be contrived about even worse failings and perversions. After an atmosphere of revulsion is created, the enemy will then move against even the most respected Evangelical, Pentecostal, Protestant, Charismatic and Catholic leaders with charges of the most base forms of perversion and ethical failures.

In conjunction with this, hoards of cults and satanic worshippers will begin attacking congregations and meetings. They will enter services en masse, spitting on people, urinating and performing lewd acts in order to humiliate the church. This practice will be publicized until it becomes a fad among the cults. What begins as a few isolated incidents will soon become common throughout the world. Again, Satan's strategy is to so utterly humiliate the church that she will retreat and go into hiding, thus thwarting the coming move of God.

It is an age old tactic of the enemy to try to devour what God is bringing forth while it is still in its infancy. We see this in Revelation 12:16 as the dragon waited for the woman to give birth so that he might devour the child. We see this principle with the birth of Moses and Satan's attempt to destroy the deliverer by destroying the male infants of Israel. This was a prophetic parallel of his strategy to destroy the infant Jesus in the same way. We also see this in his attempt to destroy a coming last day ministry through abortion, drugs, pornography, etc.

## The Purging of Leadership

The Lord is allowing this onslaught for His own purposes. He is going to have a pure and holy church. In the first century it was a noble thing to desire a position of leadership in the church. Those who did so were putting their lives and families in jeopardy. This is still true throughout much of the world.

But in the West a church leader now has more in common with a corporate executive than its Biblical counterpart. Instead of having the same mind that was in Christ Jesus, who **"emptied Himself... and became of no reputation,"** church leadership has often been used as one of the most vile forms of self-promotion. This misuse of ministry is coming to an end.

There are many sincere and devoted men of God presently serving in positions of leadership, but there are also many who have attained such positions through political manipulation and self-promotion. To these church leadership is merely another profession rather than a calling. These will not be able to stand the humiliation which is coming; they will flee, demonstrating that they were in fact hirelings, not serving in devotion to the Lord but for their own personal interests.

Some of those who were called and appointed by God will also be humiliated and found powerless at times to deal with the onslaught. Even so, these will not run, but will remain faithful to their charge. Their failures will result in a greater determination to know the truth of God's delegated authority over the evil one. By this they will be delivered from hindering delusions and begin to walk in a power and authority never before experienced. The enemy's strategy of humiliating the saints into retreat will actually work to purify the ranks and inculcate in the faithful an even greater resolve.

This humiliation will ultimately reduce many congregations and movements in the church to a figurative Gideon's three hundred. Like Gideon's little band, who could no longer stand the humiliation of Israel at the hands of Midian, these will be pushed to the limit of what they can tolerate. They will then take their little lights and trumpets (messages) and attack the entire camp of the enemy beginning the rout. After this many of those who have departed out of fear and confusion will return helping to complete the victory to bring in a great harvest. Every bit of ground lost during his onslaught will be regained and much more, all within a very short period of time.

## The Key to Our Victory

The church's posture towards this coming slander must be a determination for us to indeed humble ourselves under the mighty hand of God, not man or Satan. The Lord **"resists the proud, but gives His grace to the humble" (James 4:6).** We must not let the revelations of sin drive us into hiding but rather to the throne of grace. We need not hide from or deny the true failures, but confess them and repent of our evil ways. The Lord's ultimate victory over the accuser will be so great that the church will be esteemed and marveled at by the entire world very soon after the peak of her humiliation. But the church's exaltation will not come because we have started to look better in the sight of man, but because we will have embraced the cross and allowed the humiliation to drive us to the throne of grace, and God will then lift us up. What the world thinks of the church will have little to do with her exaltation or humiliation—God will determine her fate. The Lord is allowing this onslaught to deliver His people from the fear of man.

When the church comes out of this period, she will have a changed concept of both humility and exaltation. We will never again use the world's opinion of us as a barometer of our condition. The church's exaltation will not come from public opinion but from above. The New Jerusalem comes down from heaven; she is not lifted up from below. When we cease to care what the world thinks of us and are wholly occupied with what God thinks of us, He will then pour out a grace upon us that is irresistible even to our most vehement enemies, a grace which cannot be prevailed upon by any power of darkness.

The grace of God, purchased by the blood of Jesus, is the most powerful and irresistible force in all of creation. Through all of her trials the church is going to be so cast upon the grace of God and the power of the cross that she will walk in such power and demonstrations of the Spirit that the whole world will be shocked and even terrified for a period. The enemies of the church and the gospel, who will have exalted themselves through her humiliation, will themselves be humiliated and flee from the church in terror in the day of her power. Those who have been unjustly humiliated in the onslaught, who did not waste their trials but sought the grace of God with even more zeal, will be exalted to an unprecedented level of spiritual authority.

## An Unholy Alliance

It is important that we use this opportunity to embrace the discipline of the Lord. Nevertheless, He has us understanding **"in order that no advantage be taken of us by Satan; for** *we are not ignorant of his schemes"* (II Corinthians 2:11). As sensational as this may presently seem, there will be an unholy alliance which involves major denominations, organized crime, and even some government officials and agencies. The following is the scenario which will actually take place.

Hundreds of millions of dollars stand to be made from the slanderous articles and transfer of property resulting from the failure of major ministries. When the potential for this kind of profit exists, evil men get involved. Because of the money lost by having their publications removed from some of their more effective outlets, major pornography publishers will have a vendetta against specific ministries and Christians in general. These have been accumulating real information against some ministries; they have contrived false testimonies from paid witnesses against others. Their plan for releasing the stories is systematic and strategic for making the most on the publicity and the property transfers.

Some denominations will get involved, seeing this as a chance to eliminate what they consider "the fringe element" of Christianity. These feel that the popular evangelicals, charismatics and televangelists have deprived them of resources and support. Some of these denominational officials have no fear of God and are well aware of what they are doing. Others will honestly believe that they are doing God a favor.

Some government officials and agencies will see this humiliation of Christianity as a way to eliminate the tax exempt status of ministries (and possibly even the entire church) with popular support. This source of new income will be seen as a means of erasing the deficit without raising taxes. Major churches and ministries will be the object of audits and investigations. Many of these officials are sincere in wanting to eradicate impostors who bilk the public and the government of substantial resources. Some, hiding behind pious facades, are out to destroy the conservative Christian political clout. Others are outright antichrist. As the prophet Daniel foretold:

> **And forces from him will arise, desecrate the sanctuary fortress, and do away with the regular sacrifice. And they will set up the abomination of desolation. And by smooth words he will turn to godlessness those who act wickedly toward the covenant,** *but the people who know their God will display strength and take action. And those who have insight among the people will give understanding to the many; yet they will fall by the sword and by flame, by captivity and by plunder, for many days* **(Daniel 11:31-33).**

We live in enemy territory; **"the whole world lies in the power of the evil one" (I John 5:19).** We must not continue to judge each other by information received from the enemy's own media. It was prophesied of Jesus that **"He will delight in the fear of the Lord, and He will not judge by what His eyes see, nor make a decision by what His ears hear"** **(Isaiah 11:3).** The church must learn to walk by this same standard of spiritual perception. The love of those who do not do this will grow cold. It is time for the faithful to walk by the Spirit and to know each other only after the Spirit. Let us not be beguiled from the simplicity of devotion to Christ. We must seek first His kingdom and His purposes. Those following the Lord out of selfish ambition, who make decisions because of personal or political considerations will ultimately betray the faith and the faithful.

Those who are given understanding of the enemy's schemes will be made primary targets for entrapments in order to discredit their warnings. Some will "fall by the sword (murder) and captivity (imprisonment)". But those who know their God will not retreat; they will "display strength and take action," regardless of the consequences. This is a war and there will be casualties. Those who fall by the sword and the entrapments are martyrs to the Lord and He will keep that which they have entrusted to Him. We must not be concerned about what men, or even the church, may think of us. "The Lord knows those who are His." Those who are conformed to the image of the Lord's death, when he was alone and deserted by even His own followers, will soon come again in the power of His resurrection. Those who give their lives will be seed for the greatest victory over evil and ingathering of souls ever accomplished through the church.

This will be a period of some of the darkest and most confusing days for the faithful. Some who have appeared to be the strongest will fall. Some of these will betray many while trying to save their own lives and reputations. This has been going on since the beginning throughout much of the world, but it will be a great shock to believers in the West who are accustomed to religious freedom.

During this time paranoia would sweep the church were it not for the courage and boldness of individuals who refuse to retreat in the face of this onslaught. Some who are now considered mere "privates in God's army" are about to become some of the greatest heroes of the faith in the last day church. These will take a stand while others are retreating, refusing to be moved by any onslaught of the enemy. Their courage will give courage to a few more, who will each strengthen a few more, until the lines hold and the raging tide will be stopped. Then the entire body of Christ will go on the offensive completely routing her enemies. Then all of the fear and paranoia which the adversary of Christ used against the church will flood their own souls.

## Truth Is Stronger Than Lies

Just when it appears that the harvest is over and the spirit of antichrist has prevailed the church will rise to her greatest victory. What is left of the previous revivals will have been pruned back to only a stump, but this little stump will bring forth shoots of life that will then fill the earth. The truth will begin to burn again. Like a spark lit in a dry wood it will burn and burn until all of the wood, hay and stubble in the entire world is aflame. The little stone (of Daniel's prophecy) will strike the feet of iron and clay—the alliance of church and state. The remnants of all of the world's empires and humanistic philosophies will begin to crumble while the little rock begins to prevail in every nation on earth. Truth uttered by the faithful will impact the world like great shock waves, leveling the mountains (governments) and hills (cults and societies), raising up and empowering the oppressed.

The Lord will use the persecutions to shake the church from the dust and to prepare her for the work ahead. Persecution will separate the faithful from the false. It will help turn our theories and principles into the reality of true spiritual life. It will turn some of the most pompous and erudite Biblical expounders and theorists into spiritual beggars. Some of the most humble and ignorant believers will be transformed into giants of the faith whose steadfastness will lead multitudes into the kingdom of God.

Some of the qualities which bring men into prominence during peacetime will disqualify them when the fire comes. When the trials come we will see many of our present leaders deserting and a different class of believer will take their places. It will then require sacrifice to lead and only true servants will lay down their lives to make that sacrifice.

This is not to imply that all, or even most, members of the present leadership have presumed that position. Many are true servants and have been both called and appointed. These have not used politics and manipulation to attain their position, but have faithfully waited for God to promote them and open every door, which they walked through with fear and trembling before Him. Those who have walked uprightly during the times of compromise and self-seeking will prove to be some of the strongest leaders of all when the fire of persecution comes. But even some of the most sincere and pure in the ministry will succumb to moral and ethical failures. Many of these will be destroyed by their sins. Some, like David who fell to one of the most grievous transgressions recorded, will be restored to even greater spiritual authority.

## A Principle That Will Save Us

There is a simple spiritual principle that will help to spare us during these difficult times: **We will all reap what we have sown. We will all need grace to make it through so let us now begin to sow all of the grace that we can toward**

**others. We are all going to need the Lord's mercy so let us now begin to sow mercy.**

It is important that we not dilute the Biblical standards for discipline in dealing with sin in the church or the requirements for those whom we are to accept as leaders. But it is just as crucial that we know each other after the Spirit and not the flesh, the heart and not just externals. The Lord knew when He called David that sin was in his heart and that he would one day have a terrible fall. He loved and used David before the fall and after it. Not only did David fall to adultery but he murdered one of his most devoted and loyal men to hide it. Even this was not greater than the grace of God and after this David had a revelation of grace which may have exceeded that of any other Old Covenant prophet.

In one of the most amazing testimonies in Scripture of the grace and forgiveness of God, the Lord raised up Bathsheba's son, Solomon, to be David's heir. The Lord really can redeem even our greatest mistakes; the power of the cross to redeem is much greater than most of us perceive. In the days to come we must all become vessels of grace and restoration because we will all need it. However, we must remember that David's sin did also sow seeds in his own family that were reaped with devastating tragedy.

There is a great difference between trusting in God's grace and presuming upon it. Those who presume on the grace of God trample under foot the blood of Christ by which we were purchased. The Lord can and will redeem and forgive beyond our comprehension, but those who test the Lord by carelessly falling into sin because they presume on His mercy will bear tragic consequences. As the power of the kingdom is increasingly revealed, the consequences of sin will be even greater. When the Lord moves in power, the discipline and judgment of the Lord must likewise be more swift and unyielding, as in the case of Ananias and Sapphira. They wanted to be identified as those who were sacrificing everything while they held back part of the price. There can be no such deception when the Lord comes in power. God's grace is greater than most of us can comprehend, but let us never presume upon it.

## Misunderstanding Grace

I once attended a conference with a brother whom I have known for years would be a significant prophet to the last day church. This man has been rejected by much of the church because of the status of his marriage which has been one of many difficulties and at that time was in a state of separation. One night the Lord spoke to me in a dream about my own marriage, which I consider to be in compliance with Biblical standards. He said that this other man was more righteous in complying with His standards for marriage than I was. I had been given a godly wife who loved and sought Him and the condition of my marriage was purely the result of grace. I had given little effort to comply with His mandate in this and had been hard, unyielding and resistant to things He would have me do to improve my marriage. Against the most humiliating circumstances and resistance this other man had for years devoted himself to complying with the Biblical mandate and making his marriage work, even when he had every right, both Biblically and morally, to walk away from it. Yet, the church has judged him as a failure and me as acceptable in this area. God had a very different opinion.

This does not minimize the importance of Biblical standards, but the letter kills when it is not used by the Spirit. How many of us would have disfellowshipped David after the incident with Bathsheba, only to have later followed Absalom into deception and defeat along with the rest of Israel. Israel was led astray by Absalom because they walked after the flesh, judging by externals, instead of by the Spirit. We must seek to have the heart of Zadok the priest who did not regard

David by his successes or failures, but by the anointing and commission of God. It was said of Zadok that he remained faithful even when all of Israel went astray, and for that he was blessed and promised that his sons would minister in the presence of the Lord. These sons of Zadok were not just his natural sons, but his spiritual sons as well—those who do not judge after appearances, and have the courage to risk everything to remain faithful to God's anointed.

It is true that God's grace usually exceeds what men are able to comprehend or extend to others. Just as David was forgiven and restored after his sin, so can we be restored and healed. But just as David still had to reap what was sown, so will we. David and his family paid a terrible price for his few moments of passing pleasure. That we can be restored when we fall is a great grace, but it will be much easier for us, our families, and congregations if we resist and stand.

## Forgiveness for Betrayal

Even many who have denied and betrayed their brothers will repent and be restored. Some who have experienced the greatest weakness in denying the Lord will, like Peter, be restored and will love the Lord more because they will have been forgiven of more. These will go on to give their lives for some of the great victories of the faith. Persecution will bring paranoia upon pretenders but true believers will grow in strength and trust. These will not become closed to people because of the persecution but more open, taking greater and greater chances with their lives in order to lead others to Christ or to heal and restore the fallen. Fire purifies the gold; it burns only the wood, hay and straw. During the times of greatest hate we will see demonstrations of the greatest love; during times of the greatest fear we will see the greatest champions of faith stand strong.

Because many will stumble during these times of incredible pressure, we must distinguish between remorse and repentance. The confusion over this issue has kept the church in much bondage and weakness. Judas felt remorse; Peter repented. It is not repentance to feel bad just because we were caught, or even to *just* feel bad about the sin. Repentance is to turn away from the sin and to accept the propitiation of the cross for it.

The Lord could have forgiven Judas for his betrayal—that was not the unforgivable sin. We are probably all guilty of betraying Him; as we have done unto the least of His we have done it unto Him. What made Judas incorrigible was that he hung himself—he tried to pay the price for his own sin. Whenever we "hang ourselves" by trying to carry our own guilt, we are saying in effect that the cross was not adequate to pay for our sin and that we must pay for it ourselves. This does not strengthen our resistance to sin, it weakens it. The messages of repentance and restoration soon to permeate the church are in preparation for the dark times ahead. We must not go on hanging ourselves or others, but embrace the grace of God revealed through the cross.

Even the greatest spiritual leaders are but flesh. Peter began the church age with one of its most powerful messages, opened the door of faith to the Gentiles, and had been one of the most intimate of the Lord's disciples. Yet he had to be rebuked by Paul because **"he stood condemned"** (Galatians 2:11). He was not being straightforward about the same gospel. *Men are most vulnerable to a fall after a great spiritual victory.* Immediately after Peter had his great revelation about Jesus being the Messiah, Jesus called him "Satan" for setting his mind on man's interests (Matthew 16:13-23). Leaders stumble in many ways just like everyone else. Our faith cannot be built upon any man, doctrine, or church, but upon the Lord Himself. He alone will never disappoint us. Those who provide leadership in these times will be under the greatest pressure and will need a generous measure of grace, mercy and support from those they serve.

## Freedom and Persecution Will Change Sides

In what are presently some of the most free countries, a time is coming when the penalty for owning or possessing a Bible or religious book will be prison or death. In the parts of the world that have experienced the greatest persecution of religion, great freedom will come. Such a loss of religious freedom would seem to be a devastating blow to the gospel, but it will not thwart or even slow down its furtherance. All things do work to the good of those who love the Lord—even this.

The Bible is a most wonderful and precious gift; it is God's personal letter to us written by the blood and tears of the best men this world has ever known. However, He never meant for it to take His place in our lives. The early church did not have the Bible; if a congregation had even one scroll of an Old Testament book they were blessed. Even so, we have not even come close to approaching the power of their faith. They were dependent on a living relationship with the Lord for their guidance which is vital. Jesus did not say that when He went away He would leave us a book to lead us into all truth; He said that He would send the Holy Spirit and the Holy Spirit can never be taken away from us, even when books can. It is not just knowing the book of the Lord that should be our goal, but knowing the Lord of the book. If we know Him, losing our Bibles will not affect our faith because we have the author of the Bible living within us.

Today we have Bibles, books, tapes and a host of other aids which we must take full advantage of while we have them. Soon we will grieve over the time we wasted on worthless television programs, frivolous magazines or other diversions when we could have given ourselves to the Word.

As a preacher once remarked, "One can find ten men who will give their lives for the Bible for every one who will read it!" While we have the Bible we would do well to give our attention to it. Even so, we must guard against having our faith dependent on the letter in place of the Spirit. It was the Spirit Who was given to guide, comfort and teach us. He will continue to do His job regardless of what aids we have or do not have.

## Communist Changes and Advances

There will be many changes in communism, and the world will have a brief respite from the unrelenting assault of the red tide. It will then make some further significant advances. South Korea, the Philippines, South and Central America (including Mexico, and most of Africa) will ultimately be swept up by it. This will be such a changed form of communism that communism will not really be an appropriate word for it, but it will be economic and political totalitarianism.

There will be a period of time when the United States will have a "hot" border to the south with almost daily clashes and casualties. Internal pressures will have caused such a lack of resolve that she will even yield large sections of her own territory to invaders by failing to use the force required to stop them. At that time the enemies within will be greater than those without.

In some of the countries taken by the communists there will be an attempt to completely wipe out Christianity as well as other religions. At the same time, in some communist countries religious tolerance will increase but seldom to the degree that it could be considered true religious freedom. In the nations that remain "free" or democratic, religious intolerance will increase until believers will be in some degree of danger in every nation on earth.

# The False Church

*The most severe persecution against believers will come in countries which now enjoy religious freedom.* A number of these governments will have aligned themselves with the false church. This false church will have allegiance and authority over most of the populations of what is left of the "free world." This church will incite governments and populations against all Christians who do not submit to its authority.

The unfolding in some communist countries will have been very different. The false church will not have gained political power in most of these. Often in reaction to the false church, these governments will have given great liberty to true believers who will labor in the harvest in relative peace, their dark night already turned into day. Powerful apostolic teams will come out of Russia, China and Islamic countries giving strength to the persecuted church throughout the world.

The great changes that are sweeping the world will bring many changes to communist doctrine, theory and practice, as well as that of capitalism, free enterprise and democracy—capitalism is going to change just as radically as communism, but it will not become communistic—both will become economic and political hybrids. We must not be overly encouraged or discouraged by these changes. **"The whole world lies in the power of the evil one."** It is not communism or capitalism that is the enemy, but humanism. This includes every "ism" as they all have their root in the Tree of The Knowledge of Good and Evil.

The great changes and clashes which are coming in human philosophies will bring a more clear distinction between the light and darkness. It will be during the confusion of these times that the church will make her greatest advances in attaining the life and power in which she was called to walk.

The church will be abiding so close to her Lord during these times that she will give almost no attention to what is going on in the world, except as it may relate to opportunities for spreading the gospel.

## Chapter 11

# Preparation
# for Persecution

There will be worldwide house church, home group and "Christian community" movements which will help prepare the saints for both the persecution and the harvest. The lessons learned from many of the failed movements of the past will be understood by the new movements and used to avoid many such pitfalls.

Many Christians read the book of Acts and long for the same kind of church life. Some have allowed idealism to move them to try to duplicate it. But this kind of church life can only be duplicated if it is initiated the same way that it was in Jerusalem. The Jerusalem church experienced a wonderful community because community was *not* their emphasis. Their attention was on the Lord who was moving so powerfully among them.

As the Lord begins to move as dynamically in our midst, we too will be unified into a true community of spirit, possibly without even knowing it. The Jerusalem church met from house to house because when the Lord is moving all His people want to do is meet together and worship Him. These things happened spontaneously. There is a difference between doing something because it is a doctrine and doing it because the Lord is moving so powerfully that we are swept up in it. When the Lord is in His temple the temple will not have our attention! We will care very little about what we are doing; we will have all of our attention on the wonderful things He is doing and will move with the Pillar of Fire.

Communities and home groups that were started because of idealism or doctrines have almost all failed. Many (not all) of those which still exist are dead, continuing to exist on artificial life support instead of true spiritual life. Even though they may continue to maintain some of the vital signs, they too will expire if the machinery is removed. Many who were hurt by these failures do not want to even hear the words "Christian community," or "house church" again, but they were taken through these experiences to be used by the Lord for what is coming. Much of their revelation is in what not to do, but their experience will often save others years of time spent having to learn the same lessons. Everyone who has been through the fire of failure, who keeps seeking the Lord and pressing on, will have their failures turned into spiritual authority that will move mountains for others. Just weeks after Peter denied the Lord he testified of His Lordship with such authority that the greatest powers of his nation marveled at him. The Lord will do the same for all who just keep going and refuse to let their failures stop them.

As the intensity of this next move of God picks up, Christian communities will be birthed with people hardly realizing it. The focus of these will not be "community life," but doing all things for the sake of the gospel. The community will just be a means of becoming more efficient in the labors of the harvest. Life in the communities will be both more wonderful and more difficult than expected, but even more importantly, they will serve God's purposes.

Some communities will serve as refuges for persecuted Christians and Jews. The fear of the Lord will come upon intruders to such a degree that no one will enter their gates with impure motives. At some of these, mobs or soldiers approaching them will be struck blind or have their eyes opened to see angelic guards which will cause them to flee in panic. Those established by the Lord will be protected. This does not mean that they will not have problems, even serious ones. We have been told that it is **"through many tribulations we must enter the kingdom of God"** (Acts 14:22). In His will, tribulations are not obstacles; they are gateways into His kingdom. We are entering days when everyone will have tribulation; those who count it joy will have great joy and a peace that will cause a world in turmoil to marvel and seek after God.

As saints gather spontaneously in one another's homes and community centers home groups and home churches will be born. A great anointing will be upon these home meetings and some of the greatest visitations of the Lord will take place in them. Leaders and ministries will be raised up through them just as Stephen and Philip were in the first church. Some will even send out apostolic teams. Large congregations will begin making home meetings the center of church life. Even without knowing it most of these are being prepared for the time when all large meetings will be banned or will become the targets of violence and persecution.

## Equipping the Saints Is Not an Option

Every congregation which is not effectively "equipping the saints for the work of the ministry" will find itself being scattered and disbanded. The church will not continue to be a big sheep pen where the saints are just thrown food a couple of times a week. In the eyes of God no congregation is seen by its buildings or other works but by the maturity of its individual members.

Every ministry which has buried its talent for equipping the saints is about to have it taken away and given to those who are using theirs effectively. Many will rise and fall because of this one issue. The Lord is about to curse every "tree" which is not bearing fruit. Fruit bears the seed for reproduction. If a ministry is not reproducing itself it is not bearing fruit. Those who allow the people to depend too much on them will be judged. The Lord will not continue tolerating self-serving and self-promoting leadership. The church will soon need a thousand times the ministry it now has. This ministry must be equipped and prepared for service now.

To be distinguished from "house churches," tens of thousands of homes are being prepared for use in the harvest in another way. The Lord is even now moving upon couples to prepare their homes for basic discipleship training. The families will be trained and become effective in preaching the gospel, healing the sick, casting out demons and taking small groups of new believers through basic discipleship training as the first step toward their being incorporated into and made effective members of the body of Christ.

The massive ingathering about to come will greatly exceed the ability of any congregation to handle it without the help of these home group leaders. Regardless of their "official" training or ordination these will be true pastors, teachers and evangelists in the eyes of the Lord and those who have His discernment. Those who are led to open their homes to disciple new believers should begin to prepare for the harvest by stockpiling Bibles, basic Bible studies, teaching tapes, etc.

True discipleship will be restored to effectively prepare a great army of leaders. As the congregations are scattered by persecution, the people will be scattered abroad like seed, multiplying their fruitfulness. When a leader is removed a host will arise to take his place. Every attack against the church will result in an advance for the gospel. Preparation for this resilience is being made now and it will increase in earnest until the body of Christ assumes the seriousness and determination of an army marching to battle.

As great multitudes start coming to the Lord it is important that these are in fact being converted and are not just being swept in by the excitement. Those who are being converted to the church, personalities, doctrines, or to have their needs met will often become betrayers during persecution. A church's tendency to make it too easy for inclusion will cost many lives. We must not make it overly difficult or become suspicious of every new believer, but we must come to trust the gift of discernment of spirits and we must insist on real conversion before admittance to the holy assembly. There is only one Door to the church. We must insist that no one enter except through Him. A door is used to both let people in *and* to keep them out when necessary.

## Cults and Pop Religions

There will be an increase of cults, satanic worshippers and pop religions proclaiming the beginning of a new age. Some of these will be mere intellectual diversions while some will be fueled by demonic powers performing extraordinary supernatural wonders. Though they will capture the attention of many and often ridicule and deride the saints, they are not the greatest threat or even a significant deterrent to the move of God. In fact, some of these cults will be fertile fields from which a great harvest will be reaped. Many who are in these movements are poor in spirit, seeking spiritual answers to their problems and heart's yearnings. They have accurately perceived and rejected the shallowness of the visible church. These are seeking a reality with the power to live in these difficult times and the Lord wants to give it to them.

As stated previously, there will be attacks upon churches and congregations from satanic worshippers. They will enter meetings demanding to be baptized as a mockery and openly scorn the leaders. There will be such an onslaught of this type that it will cause many to flee from the ministry because of their fear of these confrontations. But the true ministries will soon embrace this type of confrontation because of the harvest of souls it will produce.

Our preparation for the rise of the cults should be an offensive preparation, not a defensive one. The Lord is raising up powerful young evangelists who will convert multitudes from these cults. Like Elijah, some of these will at times take a stand against a hoard of false prophets, scattering them all by the power of the One Who works in them.

Those who are commissioned by the Lord will come to a place where they are not intimidated by any spirit and will cast them out with great demonstrations of the power of God. Not only will this increase the faith of the saints but it will lead many in the world who have suffered at the hands of these cults to flee to Jesus for refuge. After a time of confrontation, those in the cults will flee in great fear at the approach of Christians and attacks from this source will then become rare.

During the initial stages of the harvest there will be a great reaping among the Jehovah's Witnesses, Mormons, Seventh Day Adventists, and other sects in which there is a doctrinal mixture. Most of these will be won by love, not truth. Some of these will become great teachers, having come to love the truth with an unquenchable zeal because of their previous delusions and bondage. Others will become tireless, faithful laborers for the harvest. The whole body of Christ will be blessed by those who come from these groups. Some will need a lot of ministry and teaching but this effort on their behalf will pay great dividends for the kingdom, just as it did with the Pharisee of Pharisees, Paul, who became the uncompromising apostle of grace.

## The Mystery of Iniquity

There are a number of "mysteries" on which the Scriptures give a great deal of understanding. There are two of which the Bible gives us little—the mystery of godliness and the mystery of iniquity. The Lord maintained these as true mysteries because of the tendency of the immature to carry them to extremes. Godliness can become iniquity when reduced to law and the iniquity of the legalistic is even more destructive than the iniquity of the carnal. Religious legalism has been the most deadly force in human history and it will continue to be a great enemy until the end.

It is not yet time to speak in depth of the "mystery of iniquity," but there are details concerning this which are generally misunderstood. Paul sheds some light on it in his letter to the Thessalonians:

> **Let no man deceive you by any means: for that day (the day of the Lord) shall not come, except there come a falling away first, and that man of sin be revealed, the son of perdition; who opposes and exalts himself above all that is called God, or that is worshipped; so that he, as God, sitteth in the temple of God, showing himself that he is God. And now you know what restrains him now, so that he might be revealed in his time. For *the mystery of iniquity is already at work*; only he who now restrains will do so until he is taken out of the way (II Thessalonians 2:3-7).**

The falling away discussed by Paul started to take place shortly after his death and continued for the next few centuries until the church was plunged into what we now historically view as the "Dark Ages." There is still a time in the last days when "the love of many will grow cold" but that is not what the apostle is referring to here. The "temple" in which the son of perdition is to take his seat is not a building, as the temple is no longer one made with hands but is in fact the church, the present temple of God.

## The Mark of the Beast

In Revelation John made an appeal to those with wisdom that they might calculate the number of the beast, **"for the number is that of a MAN, and his number is six hundred and sixty-six"** (Revelation 13:18). Since this revelation was first given to the church, Christians have been on the lookout for someone to come along and try to stamp them with a 666. This is the result of our shallow understanding of certain crucial factors which are now coming to fruition in the earth.

Whether or not this is a literal mark is *not* the important issue. Receiving a mark is not the sin. The sin is to worship the beast; the mark is merely the evidence of such worship. Will we be free of the wrath of God if we refuse to take a mark but partake of the spirit of the beast everyday? Those who are of his spirit will not be able to refuse the mark or anything else from this beast even if they know full well what it is. Likewise, if we were free from the spirit of this beast we would not take a mark, whether a literal or a metaphorical one, or anything else from him, even if we do not understand it.

True wisdom is to understand the *meaning* of that number. Six is the number of *man* (i.e. man was created on the sixth day, etc.). The three sixes indicate that this is man trying to stand in the place of the Godhead. This is the ultimate harvest of the first sin when man partook of the forbidden fruit so that he could be like God, without God. We see that this beast "comes up out of the earth" because it is the result of the "seed of Cain"—being "tillers of the ground" or *earthly minded*. If we follow the unfolding stream of every human philosophy, religion and idealogy, we can see a pattern in which they all flow together and meet at this final common position. Just as the streams which make glad the city of God all flow together and make one river of life at the end, so too will all of the streams of man's rebellion flow together in a river of death at the end.

The ultimate rebellion and mockery is for the man of sin, who is the personification of the sin of man, to take his seat in the church, the very temple of God, claiming to be the head of the church and taking Christ's rightful place. This seemingly fulfills man's ultimate ambition, which brought about the fall of man, that is to take God's place. Every church, ministry, denomination or movement which is in fact headed by men or human organization in place of Christ will easily succumb to this ultimate blasphemy. These will never suspect that this is anything but God exalting their own human effort and ingenuity. As the apostle told the intellectuals of Athens, **"human hands cannot serve Him." (Acts 17:25).** His work is not by might, power or intellectual prowess, because only the Spirit can beget that which is Spirit.

The issue of Jesus being the Head of His church will be one of the most important issue of this time. Just as the Lord's mark which He places upon His bondservants is not a literal visible mark, that which the beast is placing upon men is far more subtle than we have been led to believe. The mark of the beast is upon men's minds and their works (forehead and hands). If he does come one day with a literal mark it will only be an indication of that which he has already done in men's hearts, and those men will not refuse it even if they know what it is.

In this day the greatest threat and deception of the enemy is not coming from that which is overtly evil but from that which actually appears good and righteous. Satan's most deadly form is as the "angel of light." The fruit that brought death was from the Tree of Knowledge of Good and Evil. It is the good side of that tree with which Satan is coming to try and deceive us. Its fruit looks good and has all of the appearance of wisdom, but it kills just as surely as the evil side. It kills because it is human goodness offered as a compensation for our evil conscience, replacing the cross and therefore Jesus as our Head and the Source of our life.

To the true works of God the onslaught by the cults does not present a serious threat. It will cause some humiliations and embarrassments, but this will only work to strengthen and give greater determination to the saints. The demons quickly acknowledged and bowed the knee to Jesus and His apostles. Occasionally they would be an annoyance but not a threat. It was the most religious and upstanding citizens who persecuted and crucified the Lord and His followers. It will be the same in the days to come. The greatest persecution against the advancing church will come from the moral and conservative people and their religious institutions.

This is where the "son of perdition" will actually take his seat declaring himself to be god, an action which will be far more subtle than most are expecting. Some who call themselves Christians will consider it their duty to God and society to kill the true believers. We need not fear demons; they fear us. However, we must be wary of the spirit of religious intolerance.

The false church will have sweeping political power but its popular support will be superficial. For a time most of its attacks against true Christians will be directed against the leadership just as was the case in the first century. Then, for a time there will be such an inflow of converts that the advancing church will not be able to contain them all. Many of the former works and traditional churches will be swelled with the overflow. Because of this they will assert that they are both the cause and primary purpose for the revival.

This delusion will not last long because the tribulation in the world will eventually consume every religious institution built by man including the false church. This is the judgment of the Lord against the works He did not commission: the great "sea," or mass humanity, which they sought to rule, will rise up to destroy them. But as they are collapsing, they will attack all of the saints with great determination.

One reason the false church will begin to attack all believers is because by that time the true church's leadership will be almost indistinguishable from the general body of believers. This will not be due to the lack of leaders but because so many will have matured and begun walking in leadership. This will be the result of a fundamental departure from traditional ministry development aimed at raising up professionals to that which truly equips all of the saints to do the work of service.

Many denominations and religious institutions have been greatly used by the Lord, and will continue to be until near the end. Then the false church and large religious institutions will become the greatest opposers of true believers exceeding even the most anti-Christian governments, cults and religions. Every Christian that is in an institutional church at that time will eventually have to choose between their denomination and the Lord.

## An Unholy Alliance

There will come a great political union of many major denominations. Some of their priestly orders will be professionally trained to incite riots against believers and to manipulate governments into arresting and executing them. This will not last long because the great mass of people will turn in rage against this institution as all of the wrath which they poured out is multiplied back to them. This will all work for the Lord's purposes, separating the tares from the wheat so that they can be destroyed without hurting the wheat.

At this point we must hear a warning. The Lord said to beware of the *leaven* of the Pharisees; He did not say to beware of the Pharisees themselves. High churchmen are not our enemies; we do not war against flesh and blood but against principalities and powers in the heavenly places. As stated, there are many "nondenominational" churches which are as sectarian as any denominational church. Likewise, there are some denominational churches in which there seems to be little or no sectarian spirit. *We must stop judging each other after the flesh.* We must also stop judging congregations, movements, or ministries by externals. There will be many congregations of institutional churches that provide great leadership during the harvest. *The religious intolerance of the anti-establishment groups will prove just as deadly as that which may manifest in some institutions.*

Many of those who attack and kill believers will think they are doing God a favor, just as some of those did who carried out the Inquisitions. As the Lord Himself declared, as well as the first martyr after Him, we need to pray for the Father to forgive them because **they really do not know what they are doing**. The Lord died for them too and wants to pluck as many of them from the fire of destruction as possible. The enemy's greatest victory is to seduce a chosen vessel of the Lord. Our greatest victory is to convert a chosen vessel of the enemy, and we are going to have more and greater victories in this than will the enemy.

When the church goes on the offensive against the enemy's strongholds, it will not be done by returning slander or in the spirit of retaliation. The offensive strategy of the Lord is to bring conversion and release to the captives through the Truth Who sets all men free. We must return good for evil praying for and witnessing to our enemies of the kindness of God that calls men to repentance.

## Death Will Be Overcome by Martyrs

Every Christian is called to be a martyr whether it becomes a literal death or not. We are called to die daily. If we have truly been buried with Him in baptism then we are dead to the world. What can the world do to a dead man? It is impossible for a dead man to be offended, to feel rejected, or to fear death. This must become a reality to us in the days to come. When we perceive the riches of Christ, we will call those blessed who go on to be with Him in fullness. We will understand why **"Precious in the sight of the Lord is the death of His godly ones" (Psalm 116:15)**.

The Lord has swallowed up death in victory. It has no more sting. This reality will give rise in the church to a boldness and straightforwardness about the gospel which has rarely been seen during the gospel age. This boldness will be in striking contrast to the paranoia gripping the earth. A revelation on baptism and martyrdom is coming that will establish in believers a peace that defies all human reasoning. The death that does work in the church will result in an unprecedented outpouring of life and freedom to the world. We are here and have been called by God for this purpose.

As this day of judgment unfolds, the Scriptures will have increasingly real and immediate fulfillment. Those who seek to save their lives WILL lose them. Those who lay down their lives for the Lord's sake WILL find life that transcends their greatest expectations. Stephen was so consumed with the glory of the Lord that the stones which were meant to kill him could not even distract him. In the same way the glory of the Lord will be so great in these days that life and death on this earth will hold little significance for the saints. We will trust the Lord with our lives, the lives of our families, friends, and fellow members of the body of Christ.

In the future life will become very cheap throughout the world. Because of plagues, wars, riots and natural disasters, death will be witnessed almost daily by everyone. Burial will become as big a problem for some localities as waste removal, with fleets of trucks and armies of workers committed to the task of carrying off the dead. Nazi technology for mass disposal of bodies will be studied and implemented in some countries. Police will pay only casual attention to murders and other violent crimes taking place right in front of them. Ultimately, control will be completely lost by many governments over their populations. For a time most governments will be little more than criminal gangs who have banded together for the sake of plundering the people and protecting their own interests.

As confusion and darkness increases the peace and vision of purpose displayed by the saints will be a marvel to the world. Many saints will be killed by the authorities and mobs. Others will disperse even the largest riots by simply standing in their way and praying for the Lord's peace to calm the storm. Some will approach government compounds and forts individually and by the word of the Lord command them to disband, which they will do immediately. Companies of troops will bow to the Lord after attacking saints who stop their bullets and walk through their flame throwers. Others will believe because of the grace and honor with which the saints die. For the faithful, the laying down of this life for their Lord will be their greatest honor and those who pass from this earth will not be mourned but celebrated.

## Islam and the Harvest

Islamic terrorists will permeate the West with teams that target Christian organizations and leaders. This is in preparation for an Islamic assault upon the entire world. They will compile computer data on every Christian leader who has any kind of extra-local influence (i.e. newsletters, television or radio outreach). Their main target for attacks will be upon denominations and institutions with political influence. But they will seldom interfere with the actual harvest or true believers.

Ultimately Islam will become the greatest threat to peace, world order and freedom. This too is the Lord's doing. Just as He used the heathen nations around Israel to discipline her for idolatry and apostasy, the Lord is going to use Islam to discipline both the church and the world for its idolatry and apostasy. The power of Islam to disrupt world affairs will not be broken until there is almost universal repentance from idolatry and apostasy.

As the harvest begins to affect Islamic countries, some will vehemently resist it, but in general the harvest will reap many from Islam. Egypt will be entirely won to the Lord; her devotion and willingness to sacrifice for His purposes will be so great she will actually be called "the altar of the Lord." Some of the greatest apostles, prophets and leaders of the church will come out of Islamic countries. These will rejoice greatly in the truth that sets them free, preaching the gospel with a commitment and abandon which will inspire the entire body of Christ.

## Chapter 12

# Israel and the Church

There are dynamics involved in the division between the nations and the Jews which hold the key to reconciliation between all ethnic peoples. In His discourse about the signs of the end of the age in Matthew 24, the Lord stated, **"For nation will rise against nation, and kingdom against kingdom" (verse 7).** The Greek word translated "nation" here is *ethnos*, which does not refer to political governments with geographic boundaries which we call nations, but rather to ethnic groups.

The true sign of the end times is not just worldwide political wars, but rather an increase in ethnic conflicts. It was no accident that the Nazis were racially motivated in their conquest, and that the Jews were their main target for annihilation. Satan was and continues to be devoted to the destruction of Jewish people because he knows very well their end time destiny. Unfortunately, Satan seems to know this destiny even better than the church which shares in this destiny.

## The Coming Controversy

There will be a time of increasing controversy in the church about the place of Israel and the Jews in the plan of God. This contention will polarize much of the church into extreme positions. These positions will basically consist of those who see only the natural Jew and the nation of Israel in God's purpose to close the age and bring in the end time harvest, and those who see only spiritual Israel, the church which is composed of those who are Jews after the spirit as having a purpose in the plan of God for this day. The enemy will try to make this one of the most divisive questions confronting the last day church. Satan is not targeting this just because it is convenient but because the church's proper understanding of this issue will be crucial if she is to fully accomplish her end time mandate.

Satan has historically caused just such a controversy before the restoration of every important truth to the church. Ultimately this contention will result in a more clear revelation to the whole Body of Christ on this important and timely truth. As with most controversies there is truth on both sides. I would not presume to be able to resolve such a contention with a single chapter, especially a problem which is yet in the future for most of the church, but the issue of the end time harvest cannot effectively be addressed without including this subject.

Knowing that it is destined to be such a controversy only adds to my desire to be careful, balanced and fair in addressing this issue, but also to do it without compromise. When the enemy has an important scheme for creating division in the church it is important that we not be ignorant of it, but if possible to preempt it. The best way that we can preempt such a strategy is not by avoiding the subject, but by earnestly seeking the Lord's purposes and understanding in the matter, and resolving that, regardless of how much others may disagree with our position, we will not allow this debate to separate us from each other.

There is no Scripture which states that we must have a proper understanding of the Lord's last day purpose for Israel in order to be saved, or even to fulfill our individual callings and purposes, but the church in general will have to properly face this issue if she is to be properly prepared for her last day mandate. This last day mandate is critical because it involves the breaking down of all ethnic barriers that separate people from one another. When this ultimate dividing wall between the Jew and Gentile is brought down, the satanic schisms, misunderstandings and divisions between all ethnic groups will be stripped of their power, including the schisms and divisions within the church.

## The Test

The apostle Paul made an astonishing statement in Romans 11:28: **"from the standpoint of the gospel they [the Jews] are *enemies for your sake*".** It is important for the church to understand that the Jews are indeed enemies of the gospel, *but for our sake*. The Lord has made the Jew the greatest test of whether or not we are preaching a true gospel. Only the true gospel will move the Jews to jealousy as it was commissioned to do. The ability of our gospel to move the Jew is the acid test meant to determine if we are preaching the undiluted truth.

The Jewish mission to be enemies of the gospel was a reason for their dispersion to all nations—so that they would be there to confront and challenge the message wherever it was preached, in order to force its purity. Though it is important to win the weak and downtrodden, it is not difficult to get a decision out of a drunk in the gutter, the homeless, or the spent and disoriented prostitute. If you want to find out if you have the goods or not confront the Jew with your gospel. The Lord commanded the gospel to be preached to the Jew first, not because of favoritism, but because of the special challenge they present which is meant to make us dig deeper into the wells of salvation.

The conflict between the Jews and the gospel are meant to challenge the church to find the answers to the questions that will encompass the ultimate issues of the end times. This is why Paul made the issue of the Jew being grafted back in a centerpiece of his greatest theological discourse—the Book of Romans. When the apostolic ministry has been fully restored so will the apostolic message concerning Israel be restored. With this illumination a much greater understanding of the Lord's entire last day plan will come with such clarity that great boldness will come upon the church to prepare for and move into those purposes.

The purposes of the earthly and heavenly seeds of Abraham have set them on a collision course for this time so that neither can fulfill their calling without the other. This revelation will meet great opposition for a time, but at the right time the scales will fall from the eyes of the church and Israel on this issue. The eschatology of the church will remain veiled and controversial until that time. It is the consummation of the age when spiritual Israel and "natural" Israel become one in Christ.

## The Blessing

The Lord promised Abraham that those who blessed him and his seed would be blessed and those who cursed him would be cursed. This applies to both the spiritual and the earthly seed. Historically it seems that those who blessed the natural seed received natural blessings and those who blessed the spiritual seed received spiritual blessings. As a testimony that the purpose of God is now approaching the synthesis of the two seeds, those who bless natural Israel (the Jews) will begin receiving spiritual blessings and those who bless spiritual Israel (the church) will begin receiving natural blessings.

For example, it was because of one righteous act by Harry S. Truman, when he recognized the new state of Israel against the counsel of almost everyone in his government as well as world opinion, his home state of Missouri will be favored as a center of revival in the U.S., and his home town of Independence, MO. (Kansas City area) will become a blessing to many other nations. As a legacy to Anwar Sadat, who likewise recognized Israel against great opposition, the entire nation of Egypt will call on the name of Jesus and water the deserts of the earth with a pure gospel (see Isaiah 19:19-25).

As the day draws closer there will be an increasing release in the Spirit when we recognize God's purpose concerning Israel. This can already be witnessed in recent history. When Israel became a sovereign nation in 1948 the great Healing Revival was ignited that swept across the earth with supernatural power the scale of which had probably not been witnessed since the first century. Also one of the greatest evangelists and spiritual diplomats the church has ever produced, Billy Graham, began his ministry at that time.

In 1967 when Israel retook Jerusalem a renewal began to sweep the church and multitudes in almost every denomination began receiving the baptism of the Holy Spirit. Whenever Israel has taken territory in the natural, the church has taken territory in the spirit. It can also be noted that as disorientation and division has gripped the nation of Israel the same has pervaded the church. The church and Israel are inseparably linked in the last day purposes of God and what happens in one will be reflected in the other.

This is not to imply that the Jews have a special and acceptable position with God outside of Christ. This misguided sentimentality does not bless Israel; it works to strengthen her will to resist the gospel which she will do as long as she can stand on her own strength. The church is called to represent the spiritual kingdom that is "not of this world," and the blessings she shares with Israel must be spiritual. This is not to imply that it is wrong for nations, such as the United

States, to give Israel material aid as a nation, but the church has a higher calling—to preach the gospel, *to the Jew first.* There is no salvation outside of Christ and this must never be compromised.

## The Judgment

Because it is a central purpose of God to reveal His purposes through the destiny of the church and Israel together, there will also be an increasingly swift judgment against those who become arrogant toward the natural branches (Romans 11:18-22). This must be so because of the significance of what will happen when the two olive trees become one. The joining of the natural and heavenly seeds will ultimately result in the free interchange between the heavens and the earth, one day making it possible for God Who is Spirit to dwell on earth among men in His fullness.

For almost two millenniums God's purposes were centralized in His dealings with the Jews. Then for almost two millenniums His purpose was concentrated with the church, which is spiritual Israel or those who are Jews according to the heart (Romans 2:29). At the end of the age there is to be a joining of the two into one, through Jesus, in such a way that it will be the crowning glory of the Lord's entire testimony of redemption. As Paul so accurately foresaw, if the rejection of the Jews resulted in reconciliation for the world, then their reacceptance will actually bring life from the dead, or the beginning of the resurrection (Romans 11:15). Through this union of Israel and the church, in Jesus, there will be a release of life and power unequaled on earth since the Spirit first moved on the formless void.

The natural seed of Abraham, or the Jew according to the flesh, and the spiritual seed, the Jew according to the spirit or heart, both represent God's purposes in redemption. Similarly, the church has been torn between the two opinions of those who see the promises in heaven and those who see the redemption and restoration of the earth. Both of these positions can be verified by Scripture and both contain truth. By God's design the apparent inconsistencies cannot be resolved until we come to understand what Paul called "the mystery" of the joining together of Jew and Gentile into one. Only when we understand this joining will we comprehend God's purpose of both the heavenly calling and the redemption of the earth.

## The Last Enemy

There are many delusions that may hinder us from seeing the Lord or understanding His purposes. Racism is one of the greatest hindrances to spiritual vision because it represents the ultimate pride, pride in the flesh, and **"God is opposed to the proud, but gives His grace to the humble" (James 4:6).** The division between Jew and Gentile represents the ultimate racist barrier, and when this barrier comes down we will have overcome this greatest of human prides that has kept the world in conflict since the tower of Babel.

There is an important lesson in the reason why after the Lord's resurrection even His own disciples had a hard time recognizing Him (Luke 24:15-16, John 20:14, 21:4). The reason for this is that "He appeared in a *different form*" (Mark 16:12). This is possibly the most basic reason why we continue to miss Him and misunderstand Him: we are more dependent upon forms and formulas for recognition of one another than we are upon true spiritual discernment. If we are Pentecostal we can only recognize Him when He comes in the Pentecostal form. If we are Baptist we can only recognize Him in the Baptist form, etc. Because of this, like the men on the road to Emmaus, we too often fail to recognize Him when He tries to draw near to us. If we are going to recognize Him the barriers between Jew and Gentile, black and white, Charismatic, Pentecostal, Baptist, Methodist, Catholic, ad infinitum must all come down.

When the Lord returns He said that He was going to divide between the "sheep" and the "goats", with the sheep going on with Him to eternal life and the goats going on to judgment (Matthew 25:31-46). One of the primary characteristics He will use to distinguish between these groups is that the sheep invited Him in when He was a *foreigner* (verses 35 & 43) and the goats did not. This is obviously a most serious matter with the Lord. In fact Paul, in laying out the qualifications for elders in the church required that one be "hospitable to foreigners" (literal translation of Titus 1:8).

To be a leader in revealing God's purposes one has to love and receive those who are different because God is very different from us and He has received us. In fact, one of the primary reasons for God's blessings upon the United States has been our policy of receiving foreigners. Whether as a nation, a congregation or an individual, we can make many mistakes, but if we take care of the ones God cares for: the orphans, the widows and the foreigners, God will take care of us.

It was for this reason that Israel was commanded to "love the foreigner" (Deuteronomy 10:19); it is the natural tendency to reject and despise those who are different from us. If the Israelites were to walk with God and reveal His ways they had to receive and care for those who were different. It was much later in his discourse (chapter 31) that Moses instructed the people to teach the foreigner the ways of the Lord. We must love people before we have authority to teach them.

Love is the foundation of true spiritual authority. It was when Jesus felt compassion for the sheep that He became their shepherd. We cannot have true spiritual authority over our families unless we love them. Likewise we cannot have true spiritual authority over a city unless we love that city, or over a nation or people group unless we first love them. The divisions caused by racism are some of the greatest obstacles to the promulgation of the gospel. As stated, the harvest is the reaping of everything that has been sown and the sweeping ethnic conflicts and wars that mark the end of the age will be the reaping of the racial pride that has been sown in man throughout the ages. When the barrier between the church and Israel has been removed through Christ, each will have the spiritual authority to deal with the increasingly deadly conflicts at the end of the age.

God created a universe of incredible harmony and balance. Unity is essential through the whole creation if it is to be what it was created to be. Division brings death. The spirit of racism has been used to release more death into the world, through everything from wars and riots to serial murders, than any other single factor. One of the Lord's primary reasons for having us love those who are different is to ultimately bring down the principality of racism that is the stronghold which fortifies the position of the "spirit of death." The apostle Paul knew that when the natural branches were grafted back in, when the ultimate racial barrier between Jew and Gentile was overcome, that it would represent life from the dead, or the overcoming of death. We will not know His fullness until we lay aside the pride we have in our external forms and start to truly know one another after the spirit instead of the flesh. One of the most positive actions anyone can take for their spiritual life is to start showing hospitality to those who are different (foreigners).

Our god is a God of diversity; He even makes every snowflake different; He makes every person different. If we are going to be able to recognize His workmanship we will have to be open to diversity. One of the primary yokes keeping the world and the church in darkness is the *bondage to the familiar*. This is one of the most powerful yokes on humanity that causes us to fear anything or anyone who is different. This comes from our putting our faith in our environment rather than in the Lord. The unity the Lord is seeking to bring about in His church is not a unity of conformity but a unity of diversity. Tolerance and patience with those who are different are two of the fundamental characteristics of those who are spiritually mature.

The Jews and the church are presently intimidated by each other because they are different and because of the pride each feels in their calling. No one should ever feel pride in being called, as the apostle Paul explained:

**For consider your calling, brethren, that there were not many wise according to the flesh, not many mighty, not many noble; but God has chosen the foolish things of the world to shame the wise, and God has chosen the weak things of the world to shame the things which are strong, and the base things of the world and the despised. God has chosen, the things that are not, that He might nullify the things that are, that no one should boast before God (I Corinthians 1:26-29).**

Those who are called are called because of their inadequacy, their foolishness and their weakness. When God calls us it is to make us a slave, wholly devoted to His purposes that we should no longer live for ourselves but for Him and the world that He gave His life to save. The church is called to serve the heathen just as Israel was called to serve the Gentiles, by loving them, providing for them (a part of the tithe was actually to go to the foreigner who was in their land—see Deuteronomy 14:28-29) and being a witness of the grace of God to them. God's strength is made perfect in weakness (II Corinthians 12:9). Anyone who boasts in his calling is showing his ignorance of the ways of God. There is no pride in our calling but there is a wonderful opportunity to be a part of seeing the Lord Jesus receive the reward of His sacrifice, to know God and to draw close to Him.

As stated previously, Islam is the greatest threat to world order and to Christianity. Even so, God loves the Moslems and desires their salvation. Those who are called by God are called to become servants and we are called to serve the Moslems just like the rest of humanity. That does not mean that we support or give approval to their evil ways, but the Lord loved us and died for us even while we were still bound by evil; if we are going to be united with Him in the power of His resurrection we must also be conformed to the image of His death (Philippians 3:10).

The Western media has recently highlighted the apparent cruel and evil teachings and practices of Islam, but they have mostly been highlighting the extreme elements within Islam (just as they have with Christians, Israel and anyone else they cover). There are many devout Moslems who uphold standards of honor and integrity which exceed much that is found in Western civilization, and unfortunately, much of Christianity.

The spark that ignited the Iranian revolution was the opening of an "R" rated movie in Tehran. The Islamic people cannot comprehend how we could print "In God we trust" on our money and claim to be a Christian nation while exporting such debauchery throughout the world. They call the United States "the great Satan" because of the pornography, alcoholism, drugs and other corruption which we tolerate at home and spread abroad. Sadly, the West has in many ways earned the title "infidels." According to the Koran they are commanded to respect both Christians and Jews but when they look at our lifestyles they do not see evidence of true belief; therefore "infidel" or "non-believer" is often more fitting.

The Islamic faith will never lead to salvation because salvation is only found in Jesus, but in God's eyes, many

Moslems have been more true to the understanding that they have than we can claim to have been. The cities of Chorazin and Bethsaida were rebuked by the Lord because **"If the miracles had been performed in Tyre and Sidon which occurred in you,** *they would have repented long ago, sitting in sackcloth and ashes"* (Luke 10:13).

There are aspects of the Islamic faith that are cruel and intolerant, and many Moslems are prone to follow leaders who were cruel, pompous and tyrannical. In some lying is even considered a virtue. Even so, this is not their true nature but is a part of a survival mentality that has been inculcated in them through centuries of oppression. In general, the Arab peoples esteem honor and human dignity, and are responsive to God—they are quick to repent when confronted with the true gospel in power. They are devoted to hospitality but, they will not tolerate drugs, alcohol, pornography, stealing, or other forms of corruption. Much of what the West calls "freedom" they call license for corruption and lawlessness. Their commitment to the light that they have would shame most Christians. The same rebuke that the Lord had for the cities of Israel could be appropriately spoken in many churches today.

Arabs are not our enemies; we do not wrestle with flesh and blood but against principalities, powers and spiritual strongholds that exalt themselves against the knowledge of God (see II Corinthians 10:3-6). The church will not have any authority over Islam or any other strongholds until we begin to live by the light that we have. The cities in Israel that the Lord rebuked for not repenting *had the light* in their midst, the Lord Jesus Himself; their sin was in not responding to the light with repentance. For that reason the Lord said that it would be "more tolerable for Tyre and Sidon in the day of judgment than for them" (Luke 10:13-14). It is implied by this statement that the judgment is not so much according to the darkness but the light that is rejected. Will the Lord not apply the same standard to apply to the church?

Let us not continue to judge by the flesh, cultures and other externals, but let us live by the light that we have and seek to know others by the Spirit. When the Lord breaks down the barriers of racism and the two opposing seeds are grafted into one, such a revelation of the glory and character of God will be revealed that it will literally release the Holy Spirit in the earth with such power and life that resurrection power will be the result.

This will also mark the end of the times of the Gentiles and the beginning of the times of the Jews and Gentiles together. This represents the end of antithesis in the creation and the beginning of a synthesis of all that has fallen back into union with the purposes of God. The whole creation, that which is spirit and that which is natural will be enraptured in the love and devotion between the Father and the Son until the barriers between the natural and spiritual are removed, beginning a free interchange between the heavens and the earth. Neither will be changed in nature; that which is spirit will not become natural and vice versa. But the interchange will be free and unhindered.

The above is a scenario of **"the restoration of all things about which God spoke by the mouth of His holy prophets from ancient time"** (Acts 3:21). This revelation has not yet been fully given because it is not yet the time. Many are starting to get parts of this revelation and are carrying them to extremes which is often the result when we become dogmatic with only part of the truth (Most of the heresy in church history is the result of men taking that which God has only revealed in part and carrying it to presumed conclusions).

Because of the ultimate significance of this truth to God's purposes, Satan will soon be releasing every demon in hell to divide the church over these issues and to bring enmity between Christians and Jews. What took place in Nazi Germany will not compare to the anti-semitic and antichrist spirit soon to sweep the earth. The anti-semitic spirit will rise in the church and the antichrist spirit will rise among Jews. Both spirits will dominate the rest of the world until they promote a major attack by every religion and philosophy on earth. In time there will hardly be a person in the world not touched by the resulting conflict. Just as the Jews became the most vehement enemies of the gospel at the end of their age, many misguided Christian leaders will become enemies of this great purpose of God at the end of the times of the Gentiles. Like their Jewish counterparts in the first century, those who are so deluded will consider themselves the protectors of the true faith.

## Middle East War

As the Lord spoke through Jeremiah (16:14-16):

**Therefore behold, days are coming, declares the Lord, when it will no longer be said, As the Lord lives, who brought up the sons of Israel out of the land of Egypt, but as the Lord lives, who brought up the sons of Israel from the land of the north and from all the countries where He had banished them. For I will restore them to their own land which I gave to their fathers. Behold, I am going to send for many fishermen, declares the Lord, and they will fish for them; and afterwards I shall send for many hunters, and they will hunt them from every mountain and every hill, and from the clefts of the rocks.**

We are now in the times when the Lord has sent fishermen to call the Jews back to their land, but many have become so attached to their host countries that they will not respond to the call. There will be a conflict in the Middle East that will result in Damascus being devastated. This will be done in such a way that the world will become enraged at Israel. Many of the problems then sweeping the world will be blamed on Jews who will be holding key economic and political positions, seemingly indicating a conspiracy. Even the United States will wash its hands of Israel and participate in the new holocaust—this will be the "hunters" who drive the Jews from every nation where they have remained. This will be such a brutal persecution that the Nazi holocaust of World War II will seem like a but dress rehearsal.

During this time true believers around the world will rise to give Jews aid and shelter igniting a great persecution against Christians as well. That Jews and Christians find themselves together in this persecution is by the Lord's design. Twenty centuries of persecution and reproach has prepared the Jews for the *true* gospel. Christians who have remained faithful through these times will have the true gospel.

Christians who shelter the persecuted Jews will not give in to human, unsanctified sympathy for the Jewish troubles. These believers will earnestly confront them with the gospel with such authority and clarity confront them with the gospel that it will begin "grafting" Israel back into the true faith of Abraham. They will meet and believe their Messiah. Their two thousand years of persecution at the hands of false Christianity will help them understand true Christianity, history and the unfolding plan of God like few others can.

During this same period the nations of the former Soviet Union, in league with Iran and other Islamic nations, will march against Israel with worldwide public opinion on their side. The assault will be stopped by an earthquake and great storms. This will be so undeniably an act of God that it will also stop the assault against Christians as well, fanning the flames of revival until believers will have to hide in order to sleep because of the multitudes seeking salvation.

This will be the most glorious advance that the church is to make before the return of the Lord. The Jews and the Gentiles were meant to be one loaf (see Ephesians 2:14-18). The plan will not be complete until they are joined *in Christ.* When the times of the Gentiles end it is the beginning of the times of the Jews and the Gentiles. This period will not be complete until the barriers of race and prejudice have been overcome and there is unity between the spiritual and natural seeds of Israel.

These are major signs of the times: When anti-semitism begins to dominate the church and the world we are entering the "deep darkness" which will cover the earth (Isaiah 60:1-2). It is always darkest before the dawn; when the two olive trees are grafted into one the most terrible darkness in all of history will then begin fading into light.

During the dark period of Israel's trials two nations will courageously stand by her without succumbing to worldwide political pressure. Those nations will be Sweden and Germany. Sweden will cast off her history of neutrality and risk everything for the sake of simply doing what it right. This will so energize the nation with resolve that it will seem that the nation will have been born again in a day. Germany, having once been subjected to the terrible oppression of racial intolerance, will mobilize her political, economic and military power to stand with Israel and this world-wide onslaught.

## Chapter 13

# The Titanic
# and the Stock Market

To interpret current events in the light of Divine purpose is a primary function of the prophets. They must see the relationships between events in conjunction with the Lord's works and His message. God's prophets do not just foretell or predict but much of their ministry is devoted to the explanation of signs and messages. There are extraordinary events taking place today which do have a message for those who will hear. Two of these recent, significant events are the discovery of the Titanic on the bottom of the North Atlantic and the Stock Market Crash of 1987—and these are related.

When it was built, the Titanic was a symbol of the opulence and seeming invincibility the British Empire presumed in those days. The Titanic reflected that period's extravagance and arrogance, as well as the belief that nothing could sink the expanding world economy and British dominion. This attitude is in contrast to God's wisdom which warns: **"Pride goes before destruction and a haughty spirit before stumbling"** (Proverbs 16:18). But few considered His wisdom. No one dreamed that in just two short years the whole world would be in the flames of war and that their invincible empire was about to hit an iceberg that would ultimately send them to the same ash heap of history where every one of man's previous empires had gone.

189

Many in the British clergy encouraged the arrogance of the empire. They preached a conservative patriotism because they saw the empire as the only true protector of the faith and promulgator of the gospel. Their missionaries circled the globe to convert natives in the colonies. Their spiritual heritage was rich; British subjects who refused to compromise their convictions impacted the world with revival and reformation. They also gave the world one of its greatest spiritual gifts—the King James Version of the Bible. They could foresee no other country in the world carrying the mantle of spiritual authority that she had.

But by the turn of the century Britain had reached the zenith of her power and was beginning to regress. She was resting more on what she had accomplished than on what was left to do. Pride had replaced vision, which always portends the end. The Titanic was a message from the Lord to Britain calling her to repentance—a repentance that would enable her to continue leading the world toward the fulfillment of His purposes and would give her the opportunity to reach greater spiritual heights. She did not listen. Now she is firmly entrenched in tradition, her greatness in the past and the mantle given to another.

## The Calling of the Nation

Just as the Lord used the British Empire for a period He has used the United States in a great and wonderful way. The U.S. may have even surpassed the British in preaching the gospel, and we were used to aid in the establishment of Israel and as a primary hedge against the communist plague. By giving purpose and meaning to the value of the individual, America rose to be the greatest nation in history. When she had the power to dominate the world and dictate policy as the lone possessor of nuclear weapons our esteem for liberty and free determination would hardly consider it.

America is a nation of pioneers, more interested in going somewhere new or making something new than trying to dominate the world. The apostle exhorted us to give honor to whom honor is due; we should give a great deal to the founders of America who risked their lives, their fortunes and their sacred honor so that we could live in a land of liberty. Now, as painful as it is to see, the handwriting is on our wall. One of the most destructive things that can happen to a great nation has happened to the United States—our vision has been turned to pride. We have begun to rest more on what has been done than pressing on towards what is left to do.

## The Warning

Paul warned the Gentiles, who have been grafted into the vine because of the Jew's hardness of heart, that they too could be quickly removed by their own pride. In the same way pride can remove a nation from its position in God's purposes. He is able to raise up even the most insignificant nation to take its place. He does not need the United States; the United States needs Him. The sinking of the Titanic was a warning to the empire to repent of its arrogance, signifying that nothing man can build is invincible. Her recent discovery on the bottom of the North Atlantic is a timely reminder of just how foolish some of our present arrogance will prove to be if we do not repent of it. In the same way the space shuttle catastrophe was a warning to the United States. The glory of this nation of technological wonders was rising to the heavens one minute, and the next she was gone, exactly like the Biblical admonition: **"And I will grant wonders in the sky above, and signs on the earth beneath; blood, and fire, and vapor of smoke"** (Acts 2:19)

The nation was shocked and horrified by the blood, the fire, and vapor of smoke the Challenger burned in our hearts that day—but did we get the message? The Lord did not blow up the Challenger; it was our pride that caused it. Pride breeds carelessness. Without repentance this nation can evaporate into a few tiny little fragments just as quickly as the shuttle did. Economically we are primed for just such a disaster.

Is there no hope for the United States? Yes, if there is repentance. With every prophet and warning sent by the Lord there is an appeal for repentance. The judgments foretold come to pass only if we refuse to hear and turn from our wicked ways. There were many prophecies given in the 1970s about the impending judgment of God on America. Then there was a measure of repentance which delayed the judgment, just as we see on occasion for Biblical nations. We must not think that because the judgments did not come to pass that the prophecies were not from the Lord. On the contrary, they accomplished the necessary repentance so that the Lord could give the nation more time. The Lord will always esteem mercy over judgment.

It does not take much repentance for the Lord to relent of His intended judgment. When Abraham asked if He would spare Sodom for just ten righteous men He said that He would. The repentance experienced by the United States seemed hardly measurable to many prophets, but it was enough for the Lord to give us longer. Thankfully, He tends to be far more gracious than His prophets. If there is a measure of turning from the evil that would bring His judgment, and the Lord relents again for a period of time, are we going to be like Jonah and mourn because the Lord did not bring down His fire? Are we going to be discouraged and refuse to keep prophesying? No. Let us speak His words with boldness while praying for the people to hear and repent so that the judgments do not have to come to pass. A single soul is worth more than our pride; how much more an entire nation?

We must pray for repentance that these things will not have to come to pass now, but we know by the Biblical prophecies that some eventually will. The Lord knows the end from the beginning and He knows there will be a time when there will be no repentance. Many are saying today, "We've heard that all before and nothing happened." Few understand why nothing happened. The Scriptures are clear that times of trouble will come upon the world; we should always be ready. Let us pray for repentance but prepare for the tribulations. If it is time, we know the kingdom is that much closer, so we have cause for rejoicing either way. But we must not be like the foolish virgins who decided to sleep because the Lord seemed to delay His coming. If He gives us another year or fifty, let us use the time wisely.

## Pride Is a Time Bomb

The Lord did not sink the Titanic—pride sank her. Because they didn't think she could sink, they sailed boldly into dangerous waters with reckless abandon. This "unsinkable" pride of the Empire proved to be incredibly fragile, just like the Empire itself and just like every empire.

In relation to the present world economy, it has been repeated by many and believed by most, that what happened in 1929 could never happen again. It is said that there are too many safeguards such as a stronger Federal Reserve, higher margin requirements for speculators and institutions, FDIC, FSLIC, SIPC, etc. Do not believe it. We are now more vulnerable to a worldwide economic catastrophe than at any time in history and we are sailing along merrily in the most treacherous of seas.

Without repentance and Divine intervention the world is on a course leading to almost total economic collapse. This catastrophe will send the entire world economy staggering to the point where there will not be a secure economy again during this age. Erosion will continue with but brief reprieves until the entire world economic system has unraveled. At this time the lifestyle of even some of the more prosperous nations will then be more like the nineteenth century than the twentieth.

The Federal Reserve, FDIC and all of the other safeguards are lifeboats that may save a few but they are completely inadequate for the voyage we are on. The owners of Titanic felt that having even half the lifeboats a ship her size should have carried was superfluous. Today's leaders are sailing with the same disdain for reason while touting their ingenuity in designing a ship they think cannot sink. In October of 1987 we hit an iceberg and we are about to see just how unsinkable this ship is.

## Why History Repeats Itself

Students of history marvel at the repetitious cycles of human mistakes. Few have been able to break out of these cycles. History continues to repeat itself because we fail to learn from history, we fail to repent of our mistakes. Few have been wise enough to see anything but what they wanted to see in the trends and events taking place around them. This has also been the case with many who were called as prophets to warn the world and the church. As it was with the Biblical seers, those calling for repentance will be lonely voices. The majority who claim to be messengers will be found preaching prosperity and peace; the majority have always been more concerned about their acceptance than the truth of the message.

Those in authority, by the nature of their power, feel compelled to put the best face on problems. Only the most courageous leaders have been able to hear the warnings and take action. Empire after empire, nation after nation, organizations, companies, churches and families continue to fail because their leaders refuse to face the problems until they are beyond control.

It is amazing how the reactions of the politicians and experts after the Stock Market crash of October 1987 echoed the voices of October 1929. In some cases one wondered if they were reading from a history book! After the 1929 crash, the first response of the politicians was to point out the "underlying health of the economy". Christmas sales that year were as brisk as ever. The crash was soon almost forgotten, remembered as a curiosity more than anything else. The market even rose again briefly before it began its long slide that bottomed out in July of 1932 when the Depression actually began.

Even though it was under the surface for awhile the economy began unraveling in 1929 with the crash; the ship then began taking on water. Pressure rose for the government to take action. As much as they tried to do what Wall Street demanded, their efforts only exacerbated the problem. As it turned out the underlying health of the economy was far more fragile than anyone had foreseen.

When the Titanic hit the iceberg, there was a disconcerting jolt. Just about everyone noticed it, but after a couple of minutes the party continued. No one could imagine that in just two hours most of them would be on the bottom of the sea. The ship was so big, and all of the experts said it was unsinkable. As well as everything seems at present it is almost incomprehensible that catastrophe may be upon us. The Lord Jesus and Paul both warned us it would be just this way when it happens.

> **For as in those days which were before the flood they were eating and drinking, they were marrying and giving in marriage, until the day that Noah entered the ark ... and they did not understand until the flood came and took them all away (Matthew 24:38-39).**

**While they are saying, "Peace and safety!" then destruction will come upon them suddenly ... But you, brethren, are not in darkness, that the day should overtake you like a thief (I Thessalonians 5:3-4).**

The Stock Market is usually a thermometer which continually takes the temperature of business. It reflects the value the world puts on the economy. Occasionally it becomes a thermostat setting the direction and pace of business; when that happens it is usually catastrophic. Not since 1929 has this change come with the force it did in October 1987. It is no longer just measuring the economy, it is now dictating policy. The only time it can do this is when extreme damage control measures are required.

A good portion of the world's investors woke up on Black Monday (October 19, 1987) gripped with panic. There was little difference between that day and any other day immediately following it. As Roger Smith, the Chairman of General Motors, stated when asked about the recent turmoil on Wall Street: "We didn't just have a tummy ache here in our country; we had a genuine, certified heart attack! If you don't recognize it as a heart attack, and if you don't get on that diet and start doing your exercise, you can have another one and it could be terminal."

## The National Heart Attack

Roger Smith was right. Black Monday was a bonafide heart attack for the world's economy because the U.S. is the heart of the world economy. It was not a fatal heart attack; it was a warning that there are very serious problems. If these are not dealt with the next one could well be the big one. So far they have not been dealt with; they have hardly even been addressed.

It was a deadly presumption for the engineers to proclaim that the Titanic was unsinkable; this sowed the seeds of complacency in the leadership on the Titanic which was the single greatest reason for the disaster. Captain Smith and his crew received numerous warnings about the ice field which lay directly across their path and they did not even slow down! Even if the ship were unsinkable, to hit an iceberg head on would almost certainly cause great damage and loss of life. The only possible reason for Smith's proceeding with such disdain for the danger is a deluding false sense of security.

## The Preparation

When looking at the course of Western economic policy for the last couple of decades, one wonders what our leaders, like Smith, could possibly be thinking and how we have escaped a catastrophe for this long. The answer is that the Lord really does have His angels holding back the four winds of the earth until He completes the work in His bondservants (Revelation 7:1). The Lord is restraining impending disasters so that His people can get ready. We must not waste the time we are given.

The Bible warned that it would be like this in these days. It does not warn us just so that we can know our doom but so we can be prepared and take action. We need not fear anything if we are abiding in Christ because in Him we are delivered from the judgments of God. We are here because the greatest move of God in history is also about to take place, and we are called to be a part of that move.

It does appear we have come to the time of the greatest troubles ever known but these are also birth pangs for the coming of a new age, the one in which our King will reign. He exhorted us to know the signs of the times and to be prepared. This is not just to save ourselves but others as well.

There is much for us to do but we will not be able to save others if we are drowning ourselves.

In the near future devastating economic problems will be sweeping the world in waves. Great countries and societies will begin collapsing. Like the passengers on the Titanic, the water will lap at our ankles, then our knees; then there will be a mad rush to the highest part of the ship. It will all be in vain because the whole ship is going to sink. The entire world system is near its end. But we don't have to go down with this ship because we don't have to be on it. The Lord is now calling us to board the ONLY ship which cannot sink—the kingdom of God.

When the lifeboats began leaving the Titanic the first ones were only partially filled because most refused to leave the warmth of the ship. They just did not believe it was really sinking. By the time it was obvious that it was sinking the boats were gone. The Lord is now loading His Lifeboat. **"Today if you hear His voice, do not harden you hearts"** (Hebrews 4:7). **"Therefore, let everyone who is godly pray to Thee in a time when Thou mayest be found; surely in a flood of great waters they shall not reach Him."** (Psalm 32:6).

## The Ark

So what do we do? It may sound too simple but we must earnestly seek the Lord. I do not mean that we should seek Him for instructions as to what we should do. We must seek Him because *He is* what we should do. He is the Ark of God through Whom we will be delivered from every flood. He Himself bore the curse of our sin absorbing the judgment that was ours. If we are abiding in Him we do not have to fear the judgment against sin. This does not mean that we will not be here or will not have to endure tribulation. It does mean that even if we are called to walk through the fire, it will not burn us; the floods may come but our house will be built upon a rock which can sustain them.

For years doctrines have been preached which have lulled much of the church into a deep sleep. This was done with the assurances that those in Christ would not have to go through tribulation. Even though this teaching is contrary to the entire testimony of Scripture, many hold this doctrine to be so crucial that they consider anyone who preaches anything contrary to be a false teacher or prophet. However, would it be better to be prepared to go through tribulation and not have to, or not to be prepared and have to go through it?

Corrie ten Boom once stated: "I have been in countries where the saints are already suffering terrible persecution. In China the Christians were told, 'Don't worry, before the tribulation comes, you will be translated—raptured.' Then came a terrible persecution. Millions of Christians were tortured to death. Later I heard a Bishop from China say, sadly, 'We have failed. We should have made the people strong for persecution rather than telling them Jesus would come first.' Turning to me he said, 'You will have time. Tell the people how to be strong in times of persecution, how to stand when the tribulation comes—to stand and not faint.' "

The Lord exhorted us over and over to be ready and watching and always to be prepared. This does not necessarily imply that we should be storing food and bullets but that we should be ready to take action in season and out of season. We cannot be like the crew of the Titanic who did not think that anything adverse could happen to them because that is precisely when we are the most vulnerable.

In the Lord's discourse concerning the tribulations of the last days, He clearly states: **"Then they will deliver *you* (He is here addressing His followers) to tribulation, and will kill *you* and you will be hated by all nations on account of My name..." (Matthew 24:9).** To tell the church that she does not have to go through tribulation is contrary to the Lord's own clearly stated warning. To contradict this can be nothing less than a very strong delusion. The enemy would not give such attention to this one issue if it were not so important.

## The Rapture

The word "rapture" is not found in Scripture. It is a modern term used to describe the event which coincides with the second coming of Christ when the saints who are alive are "changed" to put on immortality and caught up to be with the Lord in the air (see I Corinthians 15:51-54 & I Thessalonians 4:15-17). It is obvious that this catching away is a literal, bodily removal from the earth to the heavenlies and that the body is changed into a spiritual body, and from that time on believers will "be with the Lord." As to this event taking place before what is popularly called "the tribulation" there is no clear Biblical reference.

The popular "pre-tribulation" theory of the rapture is not found in church history until 1830 and can be traced to the "visions, revelations and prophecies" of a single woman, Margaret McDonald from Scotland. This new theory was later popularized by Edward Irving, John Darby and later Scofield. Dr. Robert Norton, who published McDonald's revelations in his two books, acknowledged that she was the first to split the second coming of Christ into two parts (which is the effect of the pre-tribulation rapture doctrine).

Some of the exceptional preachers and teachers of the last century and a half have embraced and promulgated this doctrine. Just as many have not accepted it including such well known and respected preachers as Spurgeon, Charles Finney, George Mueller and G. Campbell Morgan and a host of contemporaries who have taken stands against this doctrine after it was promulgated. Notable reformers who preached doctrines or made inferences contrary to this theory before its release include: Martin Luther, John Wycliffe, William Tyndale, John Calvin, John Knox, Matthew Henry, Jonathan Edwards, John Wesley, George Whitfield and David Brainerd. Because of its questionable origin and the vagueness with which any position can be established by Scripture, mature leaders of the church, regardless of their position on it, have almost never used this doctrine as a test of orthodoxy.

The whole Bible is a testimony of God's deliverance and victory *through* tribulation. When the church begins to perceive the glories she will behold during the world's greatest time of trouble, she will want to stay and fight the good fight. Through the worst tribulation in history the church will prevail and begin leading the rest of creation out of its bondage. **"All things work together for good for those who love God and are called according to His purpose"** (Romans 8:28), even the great tribulation. This will be the church's finest hour and her greatest victory. **"In all things we overwhelmingly conquer through Him"** (Romans 8:37). **"He always leads us in His triumph in Christ"** (II Corinthians 2:14).

This is not the time to run—it is time for the church to draw her spiritual sword and attack the strategies and strongholds of the enemy. The doctrine of the pre-tribulation rapture has been effective in developing a retreat mentality in the church, but it will not ultimately succeed. Already this yoke is being cast off by the majority in the advancing church. As the Lord exhorted through Isaiah:

> **Arise, shine; for your light has come, and the glory of the Lord has risen upon you. For behold darkness will cover the earth, and deep darkness the peoples;** *But the Lord will rise upon you, and His glory will appear upon you* (Isaiah 60:1-2).

At the very time when the deep darkness is covering the earth the Lord's glory will be appearing upon His people. This will be the time of the greatest conflict between the light and the darkness, and the light is going to prevail. As the apostle stated **"Through many tribulations we must enter the kingdom of God"** (Acts 14:22). The tribulations are the door by which we will enter the kingdom. This is the greatest time in all of history to be alive and to serve the Lord. Prophets, saints and righteous men from the beginning have longed to see what the last generation will see. To be here and to be a part of it is one of the greatest honors that the Lord could bestow upon us. Let us seize this great opportunity!

The believer's holding to any or all of the theories concerning the timing of this event should not be a test of his commitment to truth or the Biblical testimony. Division over such doctrines only reveals our ignorance and immaturity and we must be committed to the liberty of believers to be convinced in their own hearts concerning this and other doctrines that are not clear in Scripture. Some of the theories produced by opponents of the "pre-tribulation" position are just as preposterous and destructive. Likewise, the overemphasis and defensiveness of the "pre-tribulation" position has resulted in a widespread "retreat mentality" and fatalism within the church which has been at least equally destructive.

It is not so much the "pre-tribulation rapture" theory with which we should be so concerned, but rather the retreat mentality that has so subjugated the church. It is the entire testimony of Scripture that the Lord gives His people victory over the world as a testimony of His victory over the world; He does not snatch them out of it when things get hard. That is why the appeal to every church in Revelation was to be *"overcomers."* As Christians we should always be spiritually prepared for trials and tribulations; our Armageddon may come at the next stoplight! Millions of Christians in this century went through inhuman tortures before their death for the name of Jesus. Whether it was "the" tribulation or not was of little concern to parents who watched their children starved to death because of their confession of Christ. We live in enemy territory, **"The whole world lies in the power of the evil one"** (I John 5:19).

Possibly the most bazaar, diabolical and ironic twist of all, is that, while Christians are now having their children kidnapped for human sacrifice in satanic rituals right in the U.S. and in other major Western countries, while Islam has become the fastest growing religion, with mosques now being built faster than churches throughout the world with their intent on world dominion (Islam means "submission" and their goal is to bring under submission to their doctrine), Christians actually divide over and call each other false teachers because of their position on the rapture! The angels must rank this near the top of all of the follies they have seen committed by deluded men. As the times get darker such follies will be increasingly costly to the church.

## Chapter 14

# Faultfinders
## vs.
# Leadership

According to the Biblical exhortation, it must be our commitment to **"Prove all things, holding fast to that which is good"** (I Thessalonians 5:21), *not that which is bad.* We must search out a matter thoroughly before we make judgments, looking for what is good instead of what is wrong. We must limit our judgments by the limits of our knowledge, refusing to take a stand on that which we do not understand.

As Paul Cain once stated, "Almost every heresy in the history of the church is the result of men trying to carry to logical conclusions that which God has only revealed in part." When the Lord has only clearly revealed something in part we must be content with that part, to go beyond it is to tread in dangerous waters. To be dogmatic with what we think we understand beyond the clear revelation of Scripture will almost certainly lead to destructive divisions in the church and make us stumbling blocks. These do need to be addressed, but by the appointed elders of the church, not self-appointed "heresy hunters."

Some heresy hunters have done a good work in alerting the body of Christ to serious problems and deceptions both inside and outside of the church. Many have done more damage to the church than the actual heresies they are fight-

205

ing. The tactics and deceptions of many who "preach against" certain doctrines in the name of preserving the truth, continue to cause many of the unnecessary divisions in the church, injuring the very ones they are trying to protect. Many of these, because they have become so focused on trying to find what is wrong, have taken on the very spirit of the accuser of the brethren who is the greatest enemy of the church. The free associations and overgeneralizations of those Jude called "fault finders" are a destructive force that has ensnared and destroyed the effective spiritual life and witness of larger portions of the church than possibly any single false teaching.

The Lord Himself warned that the very last thing that we want to be is a stumbling block, that it would be better for us to not even be born than to cause even one of His little ones to stumble. It will be a much more tolerable thing to come before the Lord on that day and have had some wrong understanding about certain nonessential doctrines than to stand there with our brother's blood on our hands. The callousness with which we have been prone to falsely accuse one another and overgeneralize in our references to one another's teaching or ministry is a far more serious and destructive matter in the church than many wrong teachings.

One such popular distortion of truth promulgated by those who claim to be protectors of the truth, has been the assertion that anyone who does not believe in a "pre-tribulation rapture" holds to either the dominion theology or the manifested sons doctrine. If this were true then every Christian who lived before 1830 would fall into that category, as well as most of the truly effective and esteemed ministers since then. Many who have been the victim of this type of spiritual slander have overreacted and begun to call anyone who preaches the pre-tribulation rapture of the church a deceiver. In such a way the enemy is able to bring a serious division, and he knows very well that any house divided against itself cannot stand.

We still "see through a glass darkly" and no one has yet attained complete and perfect understanding; therefore all have and probably will continue to make mistakes. Only the most deceived could claim to have never taught anything wrong, therefore all have given a wrong, or false teaching, and probably still hold to some erroneous concepts. Therefore we must all remain open to correction and a more perfect understanding. One may give a false, or erroneous teaching but not be tagged as a "false teacher," or we would all be carrying that label. We must reserve the designation of "false teacher" for those who have erroneous teachings about the *essential* precepts of the faith, such as the nature of the birth, life, atoning death and resurrection of Jesus.

## The Two Ministries

There are presently two ministries going on before the throne of God: one is intercession and the other is accusation. These are primary distinguishing characteristics of those who are walking by the Spirit of Christ and those who are of the spirit of the evil one. Jude describes both of these in his exhortation concerning the last days:

> **And about these also Enoch, in the seventh genera-tion from Adam, prophesied, saying, Behold, the Lord came with many thousands of His holy ones, to execute judgment upon all and to convict all of the ungodly of all of their ungodly deeds which they have done in an ungodly way, and** *of all the harsh things which ungodly sinners have spoken against Him.* **These are grumblers,** *finding fault,* **following after their own lusts; they speak arro-gantly, flattering people for the sake of gaining an advantage** [the manipulative, political spirit].

The Lord said that when He came to divide between the "sheep and the goats" they were divided by how they had treated Him, which was according to how they had treated His brothers. When we wrongly accuse His people we are wrongly accusing Him. The sin of causing His people to stumble is obviously one of the most serious ones that we can commit, as He said that it would be better for us not to have been born than to do it. The callousness with which we have been prone to attack those who disagree with us is frightening in its disregard of His sobering warning. As Jude continued:

> **But you, beloved, ought to remember the words that were spoken before hand by the apostles of our Lord Jesus Christ, that there were saying to you, in the last time there shall be mockers, following after their own ungodly lusts. These are the ones *who cause divisions*, worldly minded, devoid of the Spirit. But you beloved, building yourselves up on your most holy faith; praying in the Holy Spirit; KEEP YOURSELVES IN THE LOVE OF GOD, waiting anxiously for the mercy of our Lord Jesus Christ to eternal life. And have mercy on some who are doubting; save others, snatching them out of the fire; and on some have mercy with fear, hating even the garment polluted by the flesh... (Jude 14-23)**

Those who are of the nature of the evil one are the "faultfinders" Jude warned about. "Free association" and "overgeneralization" are two of Satan's most effective tools in promoting innuendo and slander in his role as "the accuser of the brethren." Faultfinders are those who "cause divisions." Those who are of the Spirit of Christ will keep themselves in the love of God, extending mercy and, like their Lord, *living to intercede, not to accuse*.

The Lord said He would distinguish between the "sheep" and the "goats" by their actions in relation to their brothers, not by their doctrines. Satan can come as an "angel of light" (i.e. a messenger who has truth). Therefore we must seek to know men by their fruit, by the spirit, not just by their doctrines or even their credentials. Those with right doctrines and a spirit of pride or accusation will usually devour far more sheep than those who just have some wrong doctrines.

Enduring tribulation has been the heritage of the true church in this age; her integrity and character through it has been a continual marvel to the world and a glory to the Lord. If we have the true fear of the Lord we need not fear anything else. The Lord clearly told us how we can build our houses on the rock that will endure the storm (Matthew 7:24-27). There are only two requirements—to hear His words and then to act on them, *but we must do both* and we must do them now. We cannot wait until the floods come. The winds are presently being restrained by the angels of the Lord, but they will not be held back forever. We must use this time wisely.

## The Coming Anarchy

The world systems and governments are already sinking. In Scripture, mountains are often symbolic of governments, and the sea speaks of the mass of humanity (Revelation 17:15, Isaiah 17:12-13). As it says in Psalm 46:2, the mountains will slip into the sea, but we shall not fear. In the days to come all governments will be melting like wax (Psalm 97:5), and for a time the shifting seas which are in great confusion and turmoil will begin washing them away.

At this same time, God's government will not be moved but will grow stronger in the earth as all others dissolve. But we must understand and remember that His kingdom is not *of* this world; it is profoundly different than the governments of this world. There is some confusion over this in the church today but it will be clarified in due time. The coming of the kingdom of God is an irresistible force. Those who are sincerely seeking Him and His glory, not just their own position and recognition, will be a part of that force.

The doctrine of the kingdom is yet to be preached. The doctrine of salvation has gone into most of the world but not the gospel of the kingdom. There may be many preaching "a" doctrine of the kingdom but we have yet to hear the message of the kingdom in the power and clarity that the Lord has prepared for the last day—but it is not far off. The coming of the kingdom is going to be far more subtle than we have been led to believe. As Jesus warned the Pharisees who had very carefully laid out their doctrines on the coming kingdom of the Messiah: **"The kingdom of God cometh not with observation"** (Luke 17:20). Presently we should have the openness and integrity of the Bereans who would patiently listen and then search the Scriptures to confirm what they heard taught.

Though we may not yet know exactly how the kingdom is coming to the earth, we know that it is and we know how to prepare for it. We can live in the kingdom now by abiding in the King. If we are abiding in Him we will be prepared for every circumstance and we will be empowered to take advantage of them for His glory.

## Three Kinds of Leadership

The tragedy of the Titanic brought to light a striking revelation of three kinds of leadership—all three of which can be seen in the world and the church today.

The first type can be seen in Captain Smith and the crew of the Titanic. They were the best from the British merchant fleet. They believed that there was not a more intelligent, experienced or knowledgeable sea captain in the Empire than Smith. Combine that with his record of never having had a single accident at sea and we have what appeared to be an unsinkable crew with an unsinkable ship. Actually, these characteristics are probably a significant contributing factor to the doom of this ship. These all fed the pride which feeds carelessness, which sooner or later usually leads to tragedy.

The Titanic's crew had never held a proper lifeboat drill. They did not have a plan for the orderly movement of passengers to the boats, and the crew did not even know how to lower them. Everything had to be planned and learned while the ship was sinking under their feet. This obviously contributed to a much greater loss of life than was necessary. Many boats were lowered only partially full, one with only twelve people, while hundreds of passengers were held below decks by the crew. The entire ship had been caught off guard by the events of that fateful night and they paid dearly for it. Will we be caught in the same position? If we are we will pay just as dearly. But we don't have to be surprised. The Lord exhorted us to know the signs of the times and not to sleep on our watch. Prophets throughout the land are now calling for *preparation;* the Lord is giving us signs in the heavens and on the earth. He is sounding His trumpet to wake us up and we must hear it.

Almost every great man of God in Scripture and history was only successful after passing through the fires of failure and defeat. Many of the elders and fathers of the faith would not trust a man until he had his "limp" (a major failure or defeat). As Alexander Solzhenitsyn declared, "Does not even biology itself teach us that perpetual well being is not good for any living thing?" Perpetual well being can open doors to a most dangerous enemy— complacency. What else can explain how the Titanic crew could receive six warnings that there were deadly icebergs directly in their path and yet they did not even slow down!

## The Danger of Overconfidence

The Bible is most candid about the failures and mistakes of even its greatest heroes. This is a message in itself. We must take heed when we think we stand, lest we fall. Even the greatest men and women of faith had defeats and failures. Even the apostle Paul could be "foiled by Satan." When we hear the testimonies of individuals and churches which claim to have never been deceived or made great mistakes, if this is declared as a boast they will be doomed to a great fall. Those who have not been wounded probably have not yet been in the fight. Such are in danger of not only getting wounded, but getting killed.

There were two other ships which played a significant role in the drama of the Titanic disaster: the Californian and the Carpathia. The captains of these ships remarkably parallel the two other prevailing types of leadership found today.

## The Danger of Being Overly Cautious

The Californian had a captain who had obviously learned something from his years of successes and failures. He was reserved and cautious, but overly cautious. The realities of life may cause us to react this way if we allow the fear of more failure to sow in us a perpetual hesitancy. Becoming overly cautious can be just as deadly as being overly confident as it proved to be in this case. When Captain Lord of the Californian heard about the ice in his path he slowed down. When he saw the ice he ordered the ship stopped and he waited for daylight. His wireless (radio) operator began warning the other ships in the area of the danger. At 7:30 p.m. her warning was received and logged by the Titanic.

The usually stormy North Atlantic was amazingly calm that night. More than one officer remarked that they had never seen the sea so tranquil. First officer Lightoller of the Titanic made this observation at the inquiry when he declared that "everything was against us." This seems to have been a resounding confirmation of the Biblical exhortation that when men cry "Peace and safety, sudden destruction will come."

This tranquility must have overcome the crew of the Californian as well. Her bridge watch saw the Titanic approaching just a few miles away and then saw her stop dead in the water. At first they thought she was taking the same precautions for the ice which they had taken. Then she started firing rockets into the air every few minutes, which is always a distress signal at sea. The crew of the California rationalized this, remarking that it must be a signal meant for another company ship which they could not see! They did not even bother to wake the wireless operator to see if he could contact the ship. Then they watched her disappear beneath the sea while telling each other as the lights dimmed that she was sailing away! Had they responded to the first distress signal the Californian may well have been able to save all of the lives that were lost.

The incredible attitude of the Californian crew is matched by much of the church today. When the final inquiry comes and the final story is told we are going to marvel at how many were in a position to save life but instead slept right through the night like Captain Lord of the Californian when he could have done so much. Rationalization is a popular shield for cowards. Were they so afraid of the ice that they decided to humor each other with unbelievable reasons for not responding to the obvious emergency? Are we going to have to ask ourselves a similar question? As our world sinks into the deep are we going to sleep when we could be saving many, or are we going to rise up and take action?

Revelation 21:8 says, "**the** *cowardly* **and unbelieving and abominable and murderers and immoral persons and sorcerers and idolaters and liars, their part will be in the lake that burns with fire and brimstone, which is the second death.**" Here cowards are lumped together with the murderers because their actions often lead to the death of others. When we can help and we don't we will be held accountable before the Lord. The Lord Jesus came to give His life for others and He has called us to follow Him with this same devotion. We may hide and save our lives during times of trouble, but we may very well by this action be putting ourselves in the most terrible jeopardy for all eternity. If we cower and seek to save our lives we will ultimately lose them just like the Lord warned. It is only by losing our own lives that we will find them. Cowards have no place in the kingdom of God. **"Those who know their God will display strength and take action" (Daniel 11:32).** If we do not display strength and take action it is obviously because we do not know Him.

## The Resolve of True Leadership

The third ship in the fateful drama of that night was the Carpathia, captained by Arthur H. Rostron. He was known for the ability to make quick decisions and to energize those who served under him. He is a wonderful example of the leadership the Lord is preparing for this day. Rostron was a pious man devoted to prayer. At 12:35 a.m. the Carpathia's wireless operator burst into his quarters to report that the Titanic had struck an iceberg. Rostron reacted in character; he immediately ordered the Carpathia turned around and full speed ahead, later asking the operator if he was sure about the report—a striking contrast to the reaction on the Californian.

Rostron then gave an masterful display of a truly prepared mind; he thought of everything and took care of every detail. He ordered the English doctor to the first class dining room, the Italian doctor to second class, the Hungarian to third class, along with every possible piece of equipment or supplies needed for the sick and wounded. He ordered different officers to different gangways instructing them to get the names of survivors to send by wireless. They prepared block and lines with chair slings for the wounded. Bowlines were secured along the ship's sides along with boat ropes and heaving lines for lifting people in chairs. All gangway doors were opened. He then directed specific officers to take charge of his present passengers and to see to their needs. All hands were to prepare coffee, soup and provisions. He then designated all officers cabin's, smoke rooms, library, etc., as accommodations for the survivors. Stewards were sent to reassure and explain to their own passengers the reason for the activity to help keep them calm.

Then Rostron turned to face the biggest problem of all— the ice. He was heading at full speed into the same field that had sunk the Titanic. To this courageous man reducing speed was out of the question, but he took every measure to reduce the risk to his own ship and passengers. He added a man to the crow's nest, put two more on the bow, one on each wing of the bridge, and he stayed there himself. His second officer, James Bisset, then noticed his captain taking one last measure which he considered the most important of all—He prayed.

At 2:45 a.m. Bisset saw the first iceberg. They steered around it and kept going. The next hour they dodged five more. At 4:00 a.m. they reached the Titanic's last called position and began picking up lifeboats. As the sun rose it revealed an astonishing sight; the sea was full of icebergs for as far as the eye could see in all directions. Even with all the lookouts the Carpathia had passed numerous icebergs which they had not even seen. No one could imagine how they missed them all except their pious captain. He knew that he had done all that he could, but he still needed the Lord's help.

The difficult rescue of the survivors was carried out with such order and discipline that peace reigned over all. The Carpathia's passengers caught the spirit of self-sacrifice from her crew. Her first class passengers gave their own quarters to survivors; others were pitching in to do all they could. On one of the darkest nights of tragedy ever experienced on the high seas the Carpathia's captain, crew and passengers stand out as bright lights of courage and heroism. They are a demonstration of what the Lord has called us to be in the night of tragedy and loss that is now falling upon the earth. Let us not sleep as some did, or be fooled by the calmness of the sea. Let us be *prepared*!

*Chapter 15*

# Summary

The magnitude of the troubles or the revival that I saw in this vision is hard to adequately express. Even so, I know that I have only been given to see a small part of the actual unfolding of these events. As stated in the introduction, I did not see the end, but my vision ended with increasing chaos and increasing revival. I feel that more of this revelation will be given in due time, but now we must give ourselves to preparation for this great harvest. In the years since this vision was first given I think that the expectation of a great harvest is almost universal, yet there seem to be very little actual preparation going on for it. It seems that the church in general has been far more content to just talk about revival than to actually do something to get ready.

There will be other words and exhortations from the Lord and carrying great authority, coming to prepare His church for the days to come. Not to presume this is all that He will be saying, but we will soon hear His prophets and teachers begin to emphasize the following.

## 1. Build Upon the Only Foundation That Can Be Laid—Jesus Himself.

Works that are built upon truths instead of The Truth will not stand in this day. Many congregations and ministries are today devastated by the slightest shaking. The works that are properly built on a relationship with Jesus will withstand the greatest trials and attacks without being moved. There will be a great emphasis on the Lord Jesus Himself in the days to come. The increasing revelation of Him will overshadow the many emphases of the past like the greater light of the sun overshadows the lessor light of the moon when it rises. The truths that have been such a distraction will begin to seem insignificant as the church begins to see Him **"in whom are hidden ALL of the treasures of wisdom and knowledge"** (Colossians 2:3).

## 2. Remove the Barriers and Facades That Separate Us From the Lord and Each Other.

We must become more intimate with Him and through Him with each other. Spiritual pride and the exaltation of men, individual truths, or works, will come under unrelenting discipline from the Lord and will soon be understood as "strange fire". Those who continue to offer it will perish from the ministry with such demonstration that a pure and holy fear of the Lord will sweep the Body of Christ. This will help the church to move into true spiritual worship and a unity that is based on that worship.

## 3. Abide in the Sabbath Rest of the Lord.

This will become an increasing emphasis and a reality as the Lord enters His temple, the church. Our growing intimacy with Him will bring a peace that will actually calm the storm of the rising sea of humanity. The intensity of the times will overwhelm any pseudo peace. We must be one with the "Lord of the Sabbath."

## 4. Heed the Spiritual Preparation That May Be Reflected in the Natural.

For example: Some have begun moving their assets into precious metals or land. This may be helpful, but it is far more important to take the spiritual land and to lay up our treasures in heaven. The Lord is seeking givers who will become channels of His supply. For these there will not be any lack. Those who hoard or do not learn to freely give may suffer increasing crisis in their earthly affairs. This is the Lord's discipline to set them free. Some who are faithful and generous givers may also experience increasing crisis in this, but it is for their preparation to become channels for the provision of many. Remember Joseph!

Some are feeling they should limit their travel to certain areas and are beginning to emphasize personal hygiene because of the AIDS epidemic. This may be helpful to a degree, but the only true deliverance from the judgments of God is to be found in Christ. Spiritual purity will automatically result in natural purity and is far more important. It alone will protect us from AIDS or any other plague.

## 5. "The Just Shall Live by Faith," Not Fear.

Fears will greatly increase in the world. Actions taken by the church because of fear will almost always prove wrong and often destructive.

Some "faith teaching" has muddied the waters to the degree that some do not even want to hear the word "faith." This frequently happens before the Lord begins a great work. A great revelation of true faith is coming; it will be an essential revelation for us to serve in these days. Some will be called to walk where angels fear to tread. KNOW that He who is in us is MUCH greater than he who is in the world. The vessels He is now preparing will walk in a boldness and confidence that will astonish a world gripped in fear. Our faith will grow as the presence of the Lord increases. True faith is the recognition of the One in whom we believe. When one truly and properly fears the Lord he will not fear anything else.

In the coming days many will exist in the miraculous on a continual basis. This will become as natural to them as the gathering of manna was to Israel. Some of the Lord's exploits on behalf of His people will be unprecedented, exceeding the greatest Biblical miracles. These will seem almost normal as they take place because the presence of the Lord will cause more wonderment than His works. He will be very close to His people in these days.

## 6. The Lord Will Soon Open Our Understanding of His Word and Purposes to a Depth Beyond Our Present Comprehension.

The "books" are yet to be "opened" as they will be. When they are our understanding of even basic truths, such as salvation, being born again, etc. will be enormously increased. This will give far more substance and depth of purpose to the entire body of Christ. The functions of the gifts and ministries will come with increasing authority and power as their confidence increases with knowledge. The spiritual dimension will become more real to the church than the natural. When the proper Foundation has been adequately laid in the church (our union and devotion to Jesus Himself), the Spirit of Revelation will be poured out as never before.

There have been many notable outpourings of the Holy Spirit, but there has always been little lasting fruit. Multitudes who met the Lord were lost again to the world; but the Lord did accomplish what He intended. Many of those brought into the kingdom remained and matured. He now has what will prove to be a strong foundation on which to build, a net to hold the catch that He has prepared for the end of the age. Through the tribulations and dry times of the last few years He has carefully been weaving strong cords that He is now beginning to bind together.

## The Chord of Three Strands

Do not resist the Lord in this work. Seek greater intimacy with the Lord, and open yourself to your fellow members in the body of Christ. Reach out to them and remove the barriers. Those who have drifted into extremes will be brought back to the course never again to be distracted from the River of Life by the little tributaries which feed it. Those who have resisted new truth will soon be diving into the River, fearless of rocks or depths. The anointing will soon break all of our yokes. The Reformation showed us the Way. The Pentecostal and Charismatic renewals began leading us on to Truth. Through the coming revival, we will begin to know Jesus as our Life. When the cord has all three strands, it will not be broken again.

This word is given for the PREPARATION of those whom the Lord desires to use. Relationships are about to be built between ministries and congregations that have feared and rejected each other in the past. He will do this in many without changing their doctrines or emphasis; He will merely cause His people to rise above such differences and worship Him in unity. As He is lifted up we will gradually begin to wonder how many concerns that were so important to us and often divided us could have had so much of our attention. As this final battle begins we are all going to be amazed, and sometimes ashamed, at those we find on our side.

It is more important to abide in Him day by day than to foresee the things which are to come. If we are abiding in Him we will be at the right place and well prepared for all that He has given us to do. Jesus did not come to show us the way; He came to BE the Way. The Holy Spirit was not sent to give us guidance; He came to BE our Guide. Deception is not just misunderstanding truth, it is not being in His will. Regardless of how accurate our vision and knowledge of the times are, if we are not in His will we can be in serious trouble. We must seek the Lord, not for what we are to do, but because HE IS WHAT WE SHOULD DO. He is the Ark given for our salvation.

This vision is not intended to advocate a great emphasis upon the future and eschatology, but rather the awareness and determination of the church not to waste a single day in drawing near to God. All of our knowledge and speculation about Armageddon will not do us any good if we meet our Armageddon at the stop light on the way to work. In the days to come it will not matter too much what we know but Who we know and how well we know Him. As the Lord Himself exhorted us, we must not be ignorant of the signs of the times, but it is of far greater importance to know the One who is in control of all of these things and to be found doing His will.

## Knowing His Voice

If we are to know His voice we must know Him. I once read an account of three shepherds who simultaneously brought their sheep to a watering hole. The herds mingled until it was impossible to tell them apart. The shepherds seemed unconcerned though it appeared that they might never be able to get the sheep sorted out again. When it was time for them to depart each shepherd took a different path and began to sing as he went. There was a huge convulsion in the mixed herd; then little streams of sheep began to follow after each shepherd until they had all separated. Though all of the shepherds were singing, the sheep each knew their own shepherd's voice.

There are many voices in the world that each lead down a different path. All of the paths may look good, but there is only one way that leads to life. We cannot follow a path; if we are walking by formulas and "how to's" we will easily be misled. We must follow Him. We must be able to distinguish His voice from all of the others even when they are all clamoring for our attention. It is not enough to know someone or to be following someone who does know His voice. Many who are in leadership will have been removed. We must each know Him for ourselves. We must each be intimate with Him. When Job lost everything but the Lord, he then understood that he didn't need anything but the Lord. Neither do we! He is everything that we need for these times and for all time.

Humble yourself under His mighty hand so that you may take part in a great exaltation. Those who allow themselves to be emptied, who lay aside all personal ambition to become of no reputation, who patiently suffer rejection and misunderstanding, will soon stir the entire world with the King's message.

We have a kingdom which cannot be shaken. This kingdom is so great and so powerful that if all of the greatest problems and tragedies were afflicted upon it at once, it may not even be enough to get the attention of a single inhabitant. In the awesome expanse of God's universe, the entire earth compares as less than a single drop of water to all of the world's oceans. Except for this tiny little speck called earth, the goodness of God dominates the universe. He is in control.

## We Have the Power

The power He has given to the least of His little ones is greater than all of the power of the enemy—He has given us His Son. The whole creation does, and always will, marvel at what He has done for us, but we seem almost oblivious to it. It is time for us to awaken. It is time for us to come to know and abide in the One who dwells within us. He must become more real to us than all of the earth's problems or attractions. Once we see Him and the kingdom He has given to us, nothing on earth will again distract us. When we see our King, all human pomp and position seems pitifully insignificant. When we see Him, that which is eternal becomes more real to us than that which is passing away. In this way our lives are steered irresistibly towards the city which has foundations; the one whose Architect AND Builder is God.